Pearls of Wisdom
2002

פניני בינה

by the Students and Faculty of
The Marsha Stern Talmudical Academy
Yeshiva University School for Boys

WRITE TOGETHER PUBLISHING
Nashville, Tennessee

Published by Write Together Publishing ™ LLC.
www.writetogether.com

ISBN 1-931718-38-5 Hardback

Title: Pearls of Wisdom 2002.
Author: Various
Subject: Literary collections, poetry

For Write Together Publishing:

Publisher: Paul Clere

Editor-in-Chief: John D. Bauman

Art Director: Bill Perkins

Publishing Coordinator: Michael Pleasant

To publish a book for your school or non-profit organization that complements your academic goals or values, vision and mission, please contact:

Write Together ™ Publishing
533 Inwood Dr.
Nashville, TN 37211

phone: 615-843-6032
fax: 928-223-4850
www.writetogether.com

About Our School

The Marsha Stern Talmudical Academy/Yeshiva University High School for Boys is dedicated to synthesizing a rigorous Torah education with a superior general studies program. We emulate Yeshiva University's Torah Umadda philosophy, uniting secular and religious studies to provide a way of life and purpose for every student. We encourage students to explore academic areas, develop relationships with other students and their teachers, and make the four years they spend at our school a time of thinking, feeling, and doing. After their time in our yeshiva, the overwhelming majority of our students learn in Eretz Yisrael, go on to college and graduate school, and then assume leadership positions in their communities.

Pearls of Wisdom Staff

Editors-in-Chief	Zevy Hamburger Simmy Siegel
Directors of Advertising	Danny Berger Zohar Kastner Max Wein
Editors and Layout Editors	Neal Davis Moshe Frances Daniel Goldmintz Eli Hamburger Mayer Kadoch Zohar Kastner Simon Papiashvilli Raffi Rosenzweig Moshe Schiffmiller
Principal	Mr. Ya'acov Sklar
Dean	Rabbi Dr. Michael Hecht
Faculty Advisor/Coordinator	Mrs. Sandra Abrams

Table of Contents

Foreword

Helping students find their stories and their unique voices is, from my perspective, our key role as writing teachers. When a student's first draft flows easily and apparently painlessly, we can rejoice with the young writer. But we will be there, too, when a student struggles or stops dead in his tracks. Our job is to help students find their way to and through writing. Whether young writers produce lumbering leviathans or succinct morsels, we can find ways to lead them forward, to take hold of their writing and generate works like *Pearls of Wisdom*.

The students who submitted original works to this year's *P'ninei Binah, Pearls of Wisdom*, produced quality, creative work. It is obvious that our students, under the supervision of Mrs. Abrams, spent endless hours writing and editing the material included in this book, and I congratulate them. As educators, we find it essential to provide our students opportunities to study and write, mentors who inspire, chances to work collaboratively, and time to pursue their own important projects.

I am immensely proud of the students' achievement, and I am confident that their dedication and love for writing will continue to thrive.

Ya'acov Sklar

Mr. Ya'acov Sklar
Principal

Note from the Editors

The second annual *P'ninei Binah*, the published version of our school's literary anthology, represents the achievements and literary prowess of the students of the Marsha Stern Talmudical Academy. We would like to thank all of the staff whose hard work and devotion made this anthology a reality. We would also like to extend a very special thank you to Mrs. Abrams, who was always there guiding us and overseeing the project. It was her dedication to us and to the publication that has ensured its success. And lastly we would like to extend a heartfelt congratulations to the students whose writings made this edition of *Pearls of Wisdom* possible.

Simmy Siegel and Zevy Hamburger
Editors-in-Chief

Student Works

פניני בינה

Hebron Now and Forever

Jeffrey Dicker, Grade 11

I took a trip three summers ago
To the land where milk and honey flow.
I arrived at dawn at the Lod airport.
The country seemed like a spacious resort.

On the second day there, my great-uncle called.
He invited me to Hebron, but at first I stalled.
I felt anticipation, excitement, panic, and fear
And, paced the hotel room with a frantic demeanor.

Should I go wearing a bullet-proof vest?
Or carry a gun like a cowboy in the Old Wild West?
Finally, I called him back to tell him yes,
And, like a machine gun, he rattled off his address.

I sat for an hour on a bulletproof bus.
I tried to relax; there was no need to fuss.
The bus rocked and rolled on the rough, rutted road.
Traveling this way was the only mode.

The only other passengers on board
Were some jaded soldiers who seemed rather bored.
Each carried a rifle across his shoulder,
Which made the young men look much older.

My great-uncle met me at the last bus stop
And immediately brought me to the souvenir shop.
He bought me a shirt that read, "Hebron now and forever."
He said, "To live in Hebron is a tremendous endeavor."

He was a tall, skinny man with a warm, sweet smile.
He took me on a tour of every last mile.
There, a sense of history came alive;
Inspiring Jewish stalwarts to survive.

Hebron was a place he was proud to call his home.
He yearns for a time when there will be s*halom*.

He made sure that this land I would not forget.
By the end of the day I was in great debt
To the man who was filled with unbelievable kindness,
Who revealed to me my incredible blindnes.
All my life, I had taken the existence of Israel for granted,
And, by the end of the day, in my head was implanted
That brave men like him have to stand guard
Over the land that, for us, our G-d has starred.

Puncture (Pardon Me)

Asher Fredman, Grade 12

Let out the air that's there
Slowly and let it squeal
The harder you push
The louder it goes (ha ha)
You try to stuff
Me into so many
Places each and
Every day the
Hole gets smaller
I lose a bit
Of me which
Escapes into the
Air and dissipates
But you don't notice
And you keep pushing
Till I twist with
Weird continuous
Irregularities but
Still you can ignore the
Symptoms and one day
I will be gone
Not in a magnificent
Pop explosion but
Simply used up
Shriveled and discarded
Another test who could not
Withstand your machinery.
Next.

Ceremony

Michael Bernstein, Grade 10

The candle–
Lit with earthly fire,
Flames licking at the stars
This magic night.

The altar–
Built with ancient stones,
Stained with ancient blood
From other days.

The knife –
Shining with evil dreams,
Slicing through air and hope,
Ominous twilight.

The ONE–
Crying dry tears from long ago,
Lying on the altar,
Staring at the knife,
Lit only by the candle
This final night.

Alternate Ending: *The Fixer*

Michael Gordon, Grade 12

Yakov sat in the gloomy coach overcome by hatred so intense his chest heaved as though the carriage were airless...

He closed his eyes, trying to block out all the horrible images of the past three years, but could not. When he opened his eyes, however, he found himself somewhere else entirely.

The room was dark and warm; a single candle burning in the center seemed to heat the entire space. In the flickering light Yakov saw a table with a silver cup and a crystal decanter of plum brandy. He could recognize the distinctive odor from across the room, remembering it from Nikolai Maximovitch's breath.

There was also something else. Someone else. A dark, unmoving shape at the far side of the room. For the first time in days, Yakov felt his anger being replaced by his oh-so-familiar fear.

"Excuse me, sir," he stammered slightly, "but who might you be and why am I here?" Silence enveloped the room for what seemed like hours. *Maybe it's a statue of some sort,* Yakov thought, *or a trick of the light.*

"The reasons for your being here will soon become clear," boomed a great, deep voice from the dark figure. "As for who *I* am..."

He stepped into the shifting light of the candle, revealing the left side of his body. He was cloaked in a long, black, buttonless great coat, woven from some fabric unknown to Yakov. He wore high black boots and thick leather gloves – black, of course. On his head he wore a solid white mask, with no holes for eyes or mouth or nose. The alabaster material covered every inch of his face. On the forehead of it was the image of a moon and an odd symbol Yakov had never seen, but which looked like an upside down horseshoe.

"The Romans called me Janus," spoke the man, his voice lowering only slightly, "though I existed long before their founder was even a pup. I was their protector and patron. God of all that comes and goes, beginnings and endings, births, milestones and deaths. I am the cycle of the seasons. I am the two-faced god. I see all that has been and all that is to be. I know the past and the future." He turned his back to Yakov, though it was not his back. It was the same as his front, his arms and boots seemed to move in the reverse direction now. All was identical, except the mask. This time, it was black, a deeper black than the rest of his apparel, with a picture of a sunburst and the letter A.

"I am history, in its purest essence," he spoke through the black mask, leaning in towards Yakov as if all the vertebrae in his back had moved to the other side. "I have seen where mankind has been and I know whither it goes. No man or woman, slave or master, scholar or layman, can avoid my careful plans.

"I am history, in its blood-red glory." His voice grew harsher now. "I am every king that has ever ruled. I am every pharaoh, tyrant, caesar or tsar that has ever commanded legions of men, sent thousands to their deaths and was worshipped as a god.

"I am an irresistible force, Yakov Shepsovitch Bok, and you are a fool to toy with me."

Yakov could barely repress his shivering. "And what is it that you want from me, Mr. Janus?"

Janus twirled around again, but this time seemed to look off into space. "I want your surrender, Bok. Nothing more. Merely accept what I am giving you." Out of an unseen pocket, Janus retrieved a small green pill. He placed it on the table next to the cup and brandy.

Yakov, eyeing the pill, began to chew on his lip. "Candy I don't need, though I thank you very much," was all he could manage to say.

Janus clenched his fists and seemed to grate his teeth, if he had any teeth to grate. "Cease this charade, Bok! You know what I offer you. Take this pill and you can end this pointless struggle. One pill and I will turn back the clock, make all this go away. You will be back in the shtetl, your wife still at your side, if you wish, and little Zhenia still alive. All this pain you have experienced will have been but a dream. I only ask that you take this pill!"

"Is there another pill, maybe, that I can choose perhaps?"

Janus, losing patience, repressed his ire and hissed at Bok. "I've tolerated this long enough, Bok. Stop your petty martyr games. There are no other pills, you have only this one choice."

Janus's anger was unnerving him, but Yakov managed to compose himself enough to speak. "What good will it do me to return home? You, history, the Russians, you'd all find me wherever I hide. And besides, I have learned too much now to ask to forget it all, if you'll pardon my saying so."

Janus, slamming his fist against the wall nearest to Yakov's head, screamed, "Just take the damn pill, you stupid Jew!"

Silence again filled the room, as if some venomous creature had been set loose and all in the vicinity stood quietly in hopes of hearing its approach.

Yakov spoke first, "And what, Mr. Janus, is that supposed to mean?"

Janus pulled himself away from Yakov and withdrew to his own corner of the room where he began to pace about.

"You know what it means, Bok. You Jews are all the same. You trudge through a pitiful existence, suffering in a world that despises you and will always despise you. You have been massacred countless times for countless eons just for being Jews. And yet you still persist in living."

"Everyone has a right to live," Yakov responded.

Janus, furious, picked up the decanter and threw it at nothing in particular. It shattered against the wall in a thousand tiny pieces.

"Why do you still spout garbage!? Do you know who I am?" He moved closer to Yakov. "I am Assyria, I am Greece, I am the Roman Legion, I am four centuries of crusades. You Jews still bleed from the wounds of my knife, and yet you refuse to accept the facts! Beyond all reason you should all have died by now!"

Janus moved inches from Yakov's face, the white mask with the moon and horseshoe burned brightly in Yakov's eyes. "Will you not just *die already!?"* Janus screamed.

And Yakov, swallowing all his fear and trepidation, managed a small whisper. "After you…" as he pulled off Janus's mask. And in that one sparkling moment, Yakov Bok, a poor miserable fixer from the shtetl, saw the face behind the mask. And he understood the truth of history.

Author's Note*: The Marxist undertones of this passage in no way represent or reflect the political beliefs of the author. They are merely an interpretation of the pro-Communist ending to* The Fixer *and make for interesting symbolism.*

“ ”

Asher Fredman, Grade 12

It has no name. Some philosophers and psychologists claim that we can only think in terms of things we have names for. I think they're wrong. Probably someone once tried to derive a name for it whose properties it resembled. It is a clear plastic tube, almost exactly a foot in length, with black caps sealing it on either end. Inside is water dyed a soothing, contemplative blue, like the water in a coral reef ten feet below the surface. Resting on top of the water is a white sphere, slightly larger than ping-pong ball. The novelty of the tube is that, when you upend it, the ball whirls rapidly to the top, in blatant defiance of gravity. It ascends with urgency that it bangs against the inner wall in its haste, producing a low humming sound. My calculus teacher says that this phenomenon is due to a slant around the orb's periphery and some sort of propeller motion. At least this is what he concluded after spending twenty minutes of our class hypnotized by it.

This tube has sat on my desk from the time when I shared a room with my younger brother to the present. Now it stands among the textbooks, college brochures, and soccer trophies. Often as I sit at my desk trying to concentrate on a math problem or my history notes, I will flip the tube back and forth, watching the sphere change direction and surge upwards. When I tire of the sphere's motion, I just stare into, and through, the water. It truly is an amazing color. If it were a Crayola crayon, I would call it "Enigmatic Blue" and stick it in between the Neon and Midnight Blue crayons. It always seems that, if I stare into the water hard enough, the answers to all the enigmas plaguing me will be revealed.

Other than a single photograph, this tube is my sole connection to my great-grandmother, who passed away. We would visit her and my father's extended family in St. Louis every fall, close to my birthday. She gave me the device as a present when I turned seven. In St. Louis, I wanted nothing more than to spend every minute with my cousins, producing talent shows, playing rugby, and sleeping all together in the basement after sliding down the stairs with a blanket. Now we are all older and have our own responsibilities, problems and needs. The azure tube is my Proustian "Madeleine," a link to a past where happiness was simply spending time with my family. Or it is just my pre-electric lava lamp.

I am willing to bet that this blue baton, within which time seems to stand still, or not exist at all, will conduct me on my journey through life. When my friends and teachers see it, they invariably ask me what it is. It's nothing, I tell them. It's a plastic tube with blue water and a white ball that disagrees with Isaac Newton. It just is, and it's beautiful.

Life Lessons

Michael Strongin, Grade 12

This past August I had the good fortune to visit some friends in Israel and tour the country. When I arrived at Heathrow Airport to board my El Al flight to Tel Aviv, I saw the gruesome headline of a terrorist attack earlier that day at Sbarro's in Jerusalem. That was the first I had heard of the attack. My heart skipped what seemed like more than a few beats – I had planned on having lunch there after my arrival in Israel.

I went to the departure lounge and tried to relax while I continued to analyze the situation. What concerned me most was not the threat to my physical well-being, since the chance of actually being the victim of an attack was remote, but the certainty that my emotional well-being would be affected. I knew I would return to America a different person, stripped of my innocence. I would no longer live in my cocoon of privilege and safety, and I was reluctant to give up the sense of security that I have always lived with as an American. As I watched the rain bang against the large glass windows that night, I also thought about the possibility that I might not make it home.

The pre-boarding experience is usually occupied with the usual humdrum activities of reading, eating, pacing, or perhaps trying to watch the inaudible television shows displayed on the airport monitors. Waiting for the plane that night was much different. As I looked around, I saw many people with tears in their eyes, some people crying, and others yelling out in concern for family and friends who had had lunch that afternoon at Sbarro's.

All of a sudden, the entire hall fell silent. *CNN World Report* had begun with the bombing as the top story of the day. No one made a sound while the latest conditions of the wounded were reported and video of the horrific scene was played. The feeling in the room was electric. Everyone, from secular Jews with tattoos and body piercings to the Haredi Jews with their long coats and hats, looked at each other and silently acknowledged that we were all one no matter how different we looked or acted. I had never felt as much a part of something as I did that night. That sense of community and belonging was something truly uplifting to have experienced. I learned that being part of a community despite its inherent risks was far more rewarding than living in what I thought was a bubble of safety.

A few hours later I boarded the plane, ironically named "Jerusalem," and settled in for the four hours of sleep I was to get that night. I looked around the cabin and saw families and businesspeople wearing relieved expressions. They were happy to be going home. As we taxied to the runway under heavily armed escort on and around the aircraft, I knew that, regardless of what lay ahead of me, I had made the right decision – to stand by my community in its time under fire.

A little more than two weeks after my safe return to America, I learned once again the importance of standing with one's community, this time as a New Yorker and as an American. A plane had struck a few floors above my father's office in the north tower of the World Trade Center. Thankfully, neither he nor anyone from his office had yet arrived that morning. The invaluable lesson I learned the night of August 9 came to mind, and I thought how being part of a larger community would strengthen me once again.

Getting Letters Published in the *New York Times*

Shalom Sokolow, Grade 9

Seeing your name in print in the greatest newspaper in the world is very exciting, especially when it is attached to a piece of your very own writing. I have had this feeling three times so far after three of my Letters to the Editor were published in the *New York Times*. People have asked me how I write my letters and why they have been published. I don't have the answer to the latter part of this question, but I can elaborate on how and why I write.

My first letter to be published in the *Times* was the first I ever wrote. I was home sick one day and decided to look at the *Times'* editorials. Their third opinion caught my attention because it regarded my favorite pastime: baseball. The editorial staff was advocating a plan that would take money from teams with higher payrolls, like the New York Yankees, and give it to teams with less money, like the Minnesota Twins, in an attempt to even out the playing field. Being a devout Yankee fan and not wanting to see George Steinbrenner's hard-earned money benefit another club, I was thoroughly opposed to the idea. I then sat down at my computer and wrote an e-mail to the editors detailing my disagreement. My 102 words conveyed the message that baseball is just like any other business and should be treated accordingly. I also made sure to include my address and phone number at the bottom of the page. Not having any expectation that my letter would ever be read, I soon virtually forgot about it. But two nights later, I came home to find a message on the answering machine from a woman who worked for the editorial page telling me to call a particular number to confirm that I would give my consent for my letter to be published in the next day's paper. More than surprised, I waited almost twenty minutes before returning the call. I spoke for several brief moments with the woman who had left me the message. She asked if my letter was an exclusive to the *Times*. After I answered in the affirmative, she informed me that, barring an unforeseeable occurrence, my letter would in fact appear the following morning. Sure enough, when I awoke on December 8, 2001, there it was in the middle of the editorial page. I was elated and, content with my submission, I started to write more frequently with hopes of being published again.

The days before Pesach, 2001, my family and I were in *Yerushalayim*. I was watching the news on *Reshet Bet* and saw the stories of five Israeli soldiers who had been killed in a motor vehicle accident near *Hevron* and an Islamic Jihad terrorist whom Israeli forces had killed by planting a bomb in a telephone booth that he frequented. Previously that day, I had ridden on the road from Modi'in to the capital, a highway that had been plagued with nighttime shooting attacks, and saw numerous shot-out windows on both sides. Late that night, while unable to sleep due to jetlag, I rattled off a heartfelt composition to that omni-listening e-mail address. I expressed my hope for peace and also mentioned my fear that the compromises that had to proceed would not be reached quickly enough. I did not tell anybody that I had written this letter, being almost certain that it was of too emotional a nature to be published. However, to my surprise, we received a call from my cousins in New York, informing us that my letter had in fact been published on *Shabbat* morning, April 7, under the heading "Passover in Israel: A Wish for Peace."

After having had this second letter published, I began to write several letters a day while still in Israel in hopes of having yet another printed. My recurring name must have caught somebody's eye at the *Times'* letter department because, after sending several more letters, I received a curt reply informing me that there is a two-month waiting period for authors to submit another letter. I would have to wait until June before they would even consider printing another one.

On the morning of June 6, 2001, I spent a free period reading op-ed pieces at nytimes.com. I knew that my two-month mandatory break was soon coming to a close. One particularly interesting piece, written by Maureen Dowd, concerned a website that tells web surfers when their favorite TV shows are getting boring. Wanting nothing else than to get another letter in, I sent a message to the e-mail address. I wrote what in hindsight seems like a silly letter—people spend too much time watching frivolous sitcoms and "over-thespian dramas," and should read books instead. This was merely one of several letters that I wrote during that period and, in fact, I thought it to be the weakest. But that night I came home to a message on the answering machine from a man who said that my letter was scheduled to appear in the next day's paper. By this time, the third in a year, I was feeling a little strange about the whole thing. Even though my mother too had heard the message, she was not fully convinced until she saw my name on the bottom right hand corner of the editorial page of June 7, 2001.

So far it has ended there. On August 6, I wrote a few additional letters, but nothing came of them. I still write occasionally but am more careful now to write only if I really have something worthwhile to say. Hopefully, soon again my words will be published in the *New York Times*.

Death, Death No More!

Mordechai Appel, Grade 11

Israel...the events flash before my very eyes,
The color so bright, so vivid.
I see the people, the faces
Then it is all gone, hopefully gone forever.

Flashbacks occurring at gloomy times,
Dreary as the events I internalized.
I beg them to go far away,
Yet ever reappearing, with me forever.

I see the melancholy crow,
The mourning almost sadly palpable.
The people stare at me,
Utter bewilderment in those bold, bad stares.

I see the crowds and police horses,
The drum just indescribable.
There is the source,
Two guarded coffins.

Ladies and Gentlemen,
The words of a eulogizer
So painstakingly stated
Over the death of two beloved parents.

Binyomin and Talia are gone, killed like ants.
Eight children left,
The Kahanes are ashen,
Wasn't Meir terrible enough?

The events pass in my neurons,
I relive the moments,
Once again death,
Unfortunately tomorrow, Israel.

Practice

Yaacov Mayer, Grade 11

Coach wants me to shoot,
And made sure I knew it—
But I am too timid to be forced to shoot the ball,
Especially with coach down my back
And the bigger high school guys on the other team.
We are going through drill and coach keeps yelling.
I am frustrated from the constant negative criticism.

It is towards the end of practice and only few drills remaining,
But the anger and frustration is growing, faster than a cheetah—
I am playing *point* guard; *passing, not shooting*,
But coach wants me to shoot,
Yelling at me so much that I can see the smoke coming from his nose.
I am nearly in tears from this excessive flak.

After practice, coach and I settle our differences.
He says that he was only yelling to help me improve.
I explain how I had been up late the previous night with my visiting
cousins—
We both understand.

That certainly was not a fun practice as a young sixth grader,
And I wish I never had experienced it.
But after about four more years of ball under my belt,
I realized that, thank G-d, the work paid off.
It was not enjoyable, but it helped me become a better player.

Mature

Bentzy Tanenbaum, Grade 11

Everything has passed by so fast,
I really had no time to reflect.
Now that I sit and think,
I wish I never had left.

Why can't I be that little boy
Who is innocent and carefree?
But, instead, I am this young adult
Whose burdens are breaking me.

I remember in the eighth grade,
When everything was light.
We would chill; friends of eight years,
We were all very tight.

Then, suddenly, without warning,
Graduation day arrived.
I knew I wouldn't see most of them again;
There was barely time to say good-bye.

The past is so powerful and safe,
Where nothing is withheld.
All surprises have been extinguished
And anticipation has been quelled.

By now I have grown older;
My life has slowly changed and passed.
But sometimes I still catch myself asking,
Why couldn't those times just last?

Take Me Out to the Ball Game

Jared Hakimi, Grade 11

"Take me out to the ball game,
Take me out to the crowd."
So begins the song
Sung by fans baseball proud.
My first Mets game
At the stadium called Shea.
It was raining all night.
It had rained all day.
My mom was there,
My sister, too.
We brought along friends,
But just a few.
I had never seen a game,
Except on T.V.
That night, a great love
Washed over me.
I didn't want soda,
I didn't want a cone.
I just wanted to watch
And be left alone.

The field was brown and green and bright.
I loved the music, the noise, the light.

Fanny

Joel I. Ryzowy, Grade 11

Eleven years old and in sixth grade,
Experiences no one wishes to know.
Life's final stroke made her remote
From her family and friends.

Eleven years old and in sixth grade,
Happy times for all that play.
Recess, a time to reduce our stress,
Yet, that day, my friend was not content.
While we laughed,
She cried from pain.
My friend had died.
Our star
Had ceased to shine.

Eleven years old and in sixth grade,
I remember, the days before
We had a fight.
Did not apologize.
Both of us were angry.

Eleven years old and in sixth grade,
Her life filled with happiness–
Gone.
Her past–a faint memory.
Her future–never to be witnessed.
Her last moments, persistent and pellucid as light.

Eleven years old and in sixth grade,
A child's hopes and dreams
Never achieved.
I, her friend, survived the pain she felt that day,
But I still feel the anguish she sensed.

Eleven years old and in sixth grade,
Her name, Fanny, my friend
Her memories and sorrow
Still present today.

Stranded

Raffi Rosenzweig, Grade 11

I walk with my big brother
To my neighbor's red house in the dark.
Even before we knock,
The dog begins to bark.
When my friend, Chris, opens the door,
The dog stares at me
As she rises from the floor.
My brother calmly pets the passing dog.
He joins his friend, disregards me,
And breaks into a jog.
Chris follows, and I am left on my own.
Blocked by the salivating beast,
I feel so alone.

"Wait!" I shout,
But they don't hear.
I feel like a spurned sailor, marooned at sea,
Deserted by my comrades
Who have forgotten me.
Why don't they realize I'm not there?
Do they not know,
Or just not care?
My feet are set, rooted in place.
The dog corners me against the door,
Loudly barking in my face.

Finally, they realize their error
And return to "rescue" me,
Chuckling at my juvenile terror.

Sitting here tonight,
I, too, am amused by my fright.
Although my trepidation has lessened at least,
I still don't like that particular beast.

Free Asssociation

Avraham Albelda, Grade 12

Something was not right, correct.
Something was bad, incorrect, wrong.
Just something to write, wrong.

Something wrought of cold, hard metal.
Mettle is the power-driving source.
Meddling in things that are not your business.
Business is good in this?

Good is objective?
Subjective is more the way.
The way is to kill the enemy?
The enemy is the killer on your heels.

The hounds of hell are biting heels.
Ninetails, Resident Evil, ouch!

Fight and cause pain, hurt.
Why?
Good, bad, ugly, how do you know?
Israel forever, end this now.

The Dream

Daniel Solomon, Grade 11

I lay down for a cool night's rest.
Past minutes four, deep grew my breath.
And into dreamland sank my mind,
Deep thoughts and hidden dreams to find.

Twisting, turning, through dark night's fright,
Eyes beholding terrible sights.
I am in school; we've just let out;
A lone man falls without a shout.

His neck is bruised, blue shirt untucked.
His mop unused; its strands unmucked.
I quickly grasp my books in hand,
That grasp which strangled yon dead man.

Found there next morn by stern-faced chief.
Suspicion borne while feelings seethe.
I come downstairs; I see them knock;
They find my books past broken lock.

They search to prove, but cannot find.
Elusive are crimes of this kind.
And I go free, for school is done,
And wake to rays of morning sun.

Star Gazing

Yosef Bronstein, Grade 11

Out at night lying on my back,
I look at the sky, a deep sea of black,
Except for the stars shining bright,
Which look like tiny points of light.

The stars are my friends of the night
That I first met at camp
During the summer.

In camp, I was always out past dark,
And I used to look up at the sky,
Awed by the stars.

People thought I was strange,
Lying on my back at midnight,
Staring up at the sky.

However, slowly, some people joined me,
And soon I was not alone at night,
Looking up at the stars.

Now I go stargazing at night
When it is dark and silent,
Mesmerized by the beauty and light
That is up in the sky.

Yo, Romeo

Moshe Kamioner, Grade 9

I heard the news
That you're out of the blues.

What's with the hiding?
Is your love abiding?

How's Juliet, our girl?
Sounds like she's a pearl.

Juliet and you are the latest rumor,
Not everybody sees it with good humor.

Why did you go to the friar's spot?
Are you and Juliet tying the knot?

Tybalt sent you a note.
Do you know what he wrote?

He has a tendency to be cruel.
Maybe he challenged you to a duel.

Go show that Prince of Cats
That he should find some other rats.

You dissed Mercutio so bad.
If I were he, I'd be mad.

Don't get hurt, hassled, or harried
'Cause with Juliet you need to get married.

To reach Juliet, just phone her.
From your pal, Moshe Kamioner.

Through the Eyes of a Director

Daniel Solomon, Grade 11

Act I, Scene i

The setting is a subterranean cavern. Fires flare spontaneously from hidden vents throughout the cave. A bubbling cauldron sits in the middle of a pentagram etched on the floor. The vapor from the pot begins to coalesce and split into three distinct clouds which begin to take on human forms. Three figures form around the cauldron, dressed in tattered garments of brown and gray. The shortest, most hunched figure slowly looks up and stares at the room from beneath a ragged cowl. She intones, "When shall we three meet again, in thunder lightning or in rain." She pulls a creeping insect from her unkempt gray hair. It squirms in her fingers for a moment, before she drops it into the cauldron. The second witch, a petite woman, glares up from studying a black dagger. "When the hurley-burley's done, when the battle's lost and won," she chants, as she cuts her palm over the pot. Blood hisses as it falls in, and the pot begins to bubble faster. The dagger follows the blood. The third witch, a tall woman with downcast eyes and a comparatively clean face, looks up timidly. She murmurs, "That will be ere the setting sun," and holds an hourglass in a polished wooden frame over the vessel. A golden glow surrounds it and it rises several feet into the air, where it hangs suspended, wreathed in steam. The first witch intones, "Where the place?" as she rips a strip off a royal blue coverlet and lets it drift into the boiling water. The second witch chants, "Upon the heath," and drops a simple, unadorned golden crown into the water. Although it is a rather ordinary crown, it is polished so that it shines. It sinks under the froth floating on top of the water with a soft *plop*. The third witch murmurs, "There to meet Macbeth," and the crown floats to the top, tarnished and pitted, no longer gleaming, with streaks of rust on its edges. The fires around the room flare up simultaneously, and then extinguish, leaving the cavern in complete darkness.

The first witch intones, "I come Gaymalkin," as the cauldron glows a dark green for a moment, illuminating her face from beneath. The second witch chants, "Paddock calls," as she is illuminated with a purple glow. The third witch shines with a pulsing red light as she whispers, "Anon." The fires ignite once again, but the sisters are gone, leaving only thick smoke which drifts toward the ceiling. Three voices can be heard to chant, "Fair is foul, and foul is fair. Hover through the fog and murky air." The motion in the cauldron subsides as the camera zooms toward the rim of the pot. Two claws lift over the lip, and an enormous scorpion pulls itself onto the rim. As big as a man's hand, it is a pure, inky black, except for its two incandescent red eyes, and a blood red tip on its lethal-looking tail. It stands quivering on the edge of the cauldron before dropping to the floor and skittering away into the darkness.

Act I, Scene v

The scene opens with Lady Macbeth in an old, dusty library. The library is decorated in dark earth tones, with old manuscripts and leather-bound books lining the walls. Lady Macbeth is sitting at a large, dark, polished mahogany desk, reading an old, moldy tome. A servant in black and silver livery enters with two letters on a silver platter. He bows as he presents them to her, and she takes them, dismissing him with a wave of her hand. Not a word is exchanged, and she doesn't look up from her book. She wears a black silk dress draped over her body, in a gothic style. Black eye shadowing and red lipstick, framed by hanging black hair, make her look a bit macabre. While holding her book open with an elbow, she cracks the seal on the first letter and reads, starting with a modulated tone which quickly rises in excitement. As she reads, she rises from her chair, absently tucking the second letter into her belt, and walks around the desk. Black streamers flutter behind her, but her dress hangs unnaturally still as she glides over to an ornately carved bookcase, still reading from the letter. The book behind her is starting to close, as books do when they're not held open. Slowly, the pages are fluttering shut. The camera shows Lady Macbeth concluding the letter in front of the bookcase, and then a shot of the book on the desk, still slowly closing. Finally it closes completely, showing a pentagram identical to the one on the floor in the first scene, etched in silver, with red lettering all around and inside of it. Another shot of the bookshelf shows that the room is empty, and Lady Macbeth is gone.

The scene changes to show her walking down a spiraling stone staircase lit by flickering torches. She reaches the bottom in front of an arch carved with imps and devils. Beyond the arch is complete darkness. As she crosses the threshold, fires abruptly spring to life, illuminating that same subterranean cavern from the first scene. Lady Macbeth crosses a room to a large desk carved from black basalt rock. She places Macbeth's letter down next to a human skull. The desk is littered with other such tokens such as stuffed bats and vials filled with different colored potions. She opens the other letter and scans it quickly, stating, "So, the raven himself is hoarse that croaks the fatal entrance of Duncan under my battlements." She walks over to where the cauldron stands, bubbling quietly. She throws a handful of powder into the pot from a bag at her belt, and the cauldron bubbles furiously, throwing off waves of green, dark purple, and red smoke. She begins to recite, "Come you spirits…" as the smoke begins to swirl in a spiral around her body. The smoke whirls faster and tighter as her voice rises until she is screaming the words "Hold, Hold," and the smoke obscures her in a violent tornado of flashing colors. Unnoticed above her, the hourglass slowly spills its grains from the upper half to the lower.

The camera cuts back to the library where Macbeth has just entered. Although he has already removed his armor, he is still covered in a shirt of light chain mail over a leather vest. His coif is lowered around his shoulders. As he calls out for his lady, the camera focuses on the book with the pentagram. In a quick, subdued flash of light, it changes from an old moldy tome to a leather-bound album, as simple as the other books throughout the library. An orange cat with distinctive brown stripes darts into the room and entwines itself around Macbeth's ankles. He falls into a chair with a laugh and picks up the cat to scratch its head. Behind him, the special bookcase is silently swinging open.

The camera zooms in behind Macbeth as a dark figure glides toward him unnoticed. A black-nailed hand reaches toward his neck, and he gives a start, twisting around to stare upward in shock. Lady Macbeth smiles down at him, as the cat hisses then runs out of the room, howling. As the cat passes by that unique bookcase, two red eyes glare out from a space between two books, and the evil black scorpion quickly scuttles after the cat. Lady Macbeth begins, "Great Glamis…" and Macbeth listens. Yet the moment she speaks, "Look like th' innocent flower,/ But be the serpent under 't," he looks shocked, and stares at her with wide eyes. He seems at a loss for words when he says breathlessly, "We shall speak of this later."

Act I, Scene vi

Duncan proclaims, "This castle hath a pleasant seat. The air/ nimbly and sweetly recommends itself/ Unto our gentle senses." He takes a deep breath of fresh air. His polished crown, identical to the one in the first scene, appears tarnished for a moment, but then gleams again. As he enters the castle, the vigilant cat slowly follows him. Looking at Lady Macbeth, Duncan continues, "See, see our honored hostess…And thank us for your trouble." At this time, the cat sights the scorpion and rushes toward it. They scuffle as Lady Macbeth says, "All our service." When she says, "In every point twice done," the red-tipped stinger draws back and quickly whips forward, twice, into the cat's neck. Lady Macbeth says, "and then done double," as the cat staggers away, meowing pitifully, and the scorpion scuttles under a bush. The scene continues until the words, "By your leave, Hostess," are spoken. At that moment, the cat finally stops thrashing and lies still on the ground.

Act I, Scene vii

Macbeth recites his lines, his voice rising and falling in agitation. His facial expression alters from focused to regretful, anger to indignation. Lady Macbeth enters and he speaks his next few lines firmly, resolved not to do anything rash. Lady Macbeth looks aghast. Her voice is tinged with contempt and indignation as she begins, "Was the hope drunk…" Macbeth says, "Prithee thee, I dare do all that may become a man. Who dares do more is none." As he says that last sentence, Lady Macbeth self-consciously covers her left wrist, on which is etched a dark tattoo of a pentagram. She looks slightly taken aback, unsure of her position, but then a newfound hardness enters her voice as she recounts, "I have given suck…" As she speaks, she has a flashback of nursing a baby against her breast, of smiling down at the baby. Then her face hardens, and she raises the baby over the simmering cauldron with clawed hands. A camera shot shows Lady Macbeth's dark, expressionless eyes as the baby's wails increase and increase until they suddenly cease. Her eyes never change. The cauldron boils furiously and spews a cloudy steam, which forms the three sisters. The eldest opens her mouth to speak as the picture fades back to Lady Macbeth and Macbeth. As Macbeth says, "Bring forth men children only…" the camera shows Duncan retiring to his rooms, with the scorpion following him, its claws clicking ominously. They enter his room, and he walks past the bed on which lies the blue coverlet from the first scene.

Act II, Scene 1

The scene begins and, as Macbeth says, "I go and it is done," the camera shows the magical hourglass, with its last grains slipping through the funnel, disappearing in a flash. The flash fades into a scene of the scorpion creeping up Duncan's sheets. Macbeth walks dazedly up the staircase to Duncan's room, following the imaginary dagger, his own held out horizontally before him. A short, sharp cry emanates from the room, followed by a thrashing sound, which quickly fades into silence. Macbeth doesn't even notice, but continues into the dark room. Sounds of violent motion and rending flesh ensue, and the splattering of blood is clearly heard. A thin rivulet of blood runs from the room through a crack in two stones.

Act II, Scene ii

Lady Macbeth begins her lines nervously. The scorpion begins to scuttle out of the room, but stops to drink from the rivulet. As it drinks, it begins to swell, and grow larger. Scales expand to cover it in a jet-black armor. Macbeth exits the room, his arms covered in blood, his face, chest, and thighs splattered liberally with more. He begins to descend the stairs, and his boot falls heavily on the growing scorpion, crushing it in a shower of *cracks* and *splats*. It lets out a shriek even as it seems to melt, and sizzles until only a mist remains, which quickly dissipates. The shriek coincides with Lady Macbeth's line "Hark!-Peace." After these words comes a shot of the three sisters, each of them looking up with a startled expression in her eyes. Their shocked countenances last only for a moment before they slowly shake their heads and look down, disappointing frowns appearing on their faces.

The first scene foreshadows the entire play. Each of the items corresponds to a different component in the murder of Duncan. It should have happened that the scorpion killed Duncan, but Lady Macbeth misinterpreted the witches' message in Act 1, scene v. By her clothes and actions, she is shown to be the evil figure. She convinces Macbeth to commit murder against his will, which places the blame of the ensuing tragedy on her. The way she hides her dark actions, such as covering her wrist and hiding her "magic room" underground, shows that Macbeth has no idea of her association with the dark arts.

This interpretation fits well into the lines of the play. The viewpoint is not associated with any previous idea, lending the production an air of originality, yet it maintains the essence and spirit of Shakespeare.

Can't Decide

Moshe Kanarfogel, Grade 10

Every day people make decisions regarding all,
Sometimes a big decision, sometimes small.
It can be hard to decide which choice is correct,
Never knowing whom your choice will affect.

Do you choose what's best for others or just yourself?
Do you choose what's best for happiness or just for wealth?
Are you careful, analyzing when you must decide?
Or do you randomly choose, going along for the ride?

People lean to one side; it looks like more fun,
Not stopping to think what's good in the long run.
It's not always easy to make the right choices,
But you always must consider and listen to both voices.

It's okay to ask for help and hear what people say.
But don't automatically decide that specific way.
When making crucial decisions, try to be smart;
Regardless of what people say, the answers are in your heart.

Alone

Shimon Rosenbaum, Grade 12

No one is listening when you tell them how you feel,
You can't handle the world; you just can't deal.
You want to pack up your things and run away,
It doesn't matter where you'll go or where you'll stay.
You want to scream and yell in a crowded room
How you think your life is in impending doom.
No one's listening; no one can hear what you're crying.
You want to curl up in a ball; in your bed you'll be lying.
You feel horrible, like your world is coming to an end,
Until you realize people are listening, like your family and friends.

Moving

Avi Muschel, Grade 11

We moved into our house
Over two years ago.
It was not our fault;
The builder was really slow.
We had no house
Or place to live.
We asked our family
For their house to give.
So it remained for a year and a half;
Our family knew one day we'd laugh.

We are spending the first ten months
Of our displaced time in a tiny rented house.
We are crammed for space.
Our kitchen can't fit all the members of our family
And family dinners are a real struggle.
It's like being sardines stuck in a can.
We realize that one day we will make many jokes
About this situation.

Soon it was time for my bar mitzvah,
A major milestone and life endeavor.
Still we had no home.
And from our friends we needed a favor.

I arrive at our friend's house.
It is Friday afternoon.
There are presents, balloons and flowers all around.
I feel a little weird that I'm not in my own house,
But that's the way things are.
I cannot change the past.
Nonetheless, it is a successful weekend.

Soon afterwards all the moving is done,
With the help from everyone.
We've had our experiences
Traveling on the road.
But now we are done,
Secure in our abode.

Decision

Bentzy Tanenbaum, Grade 11

If you just think it through,
You'll realize what's to lose.
Go seek out the truth
That's all you have to do.

It's much harder than is said.
But, on the contrary,
It's all up in your head.
It's not that difficult.

Take a short time out.
Get a grip of yourself.
Think what life's about,
And you're on your way.

When the time will arrive,
Which will happen eventually,
You must prepare to decide
Which road you will take.

Help

Moshe Frances, Grade 12

What is happening?
The world is turning, running away from me,
And I can't keep up.
Where is everyone going?
People talk to me, but I can't respond.
My head is throbbing.
My hand is shaking.
I can't stop now.
I'll never make it.
I stare wordlessly at the sky;
I remain asleep,
Unconscious and unmoving.

A Cat's Life

Elyada Goldwicht, Grade 10

Feline grace with a fashionable face,
Distant to one and all.
Slanted eyes, happy sighs
Curled up in my front hall.
Fur-like silk drinks up her milk
As if it were G-d's nectar.
Paws open out as catnip whirls—
Her high a heady image.
Chasing mice is kind of nice.
A huntress brave and strong
Bows her head above the dead,
Meowing victory strong.
On the sill she poses, still,
A statue of such beauty.
Sees a fly come flying by,
Attacks for it's her duty.
No one cares or understands
That she seems to live with
Carefree days and selfish ways…
A purr-fect life, no doubt.

In Out In Out

Michael Bernstein, Grade 10

Inside strange.
Outside hate.
In where?
In me.
Out where?
Out there.

A Doctor's Language

Moshe Schiffmiller, Grade 10

You think it's English,
But it isn't.

It's their code,
A trade secret.

You don't know the terms,
That's the whole point.

It's what makes them above all the other professionals,
Besides their knowledge.

To rebel,
One must learn their language and infiltrate their club.

Find out what a GSW is,
Or a CBC with Differentials,
Or a Chem. 20,
Or an ABG,
Or an EKG,
Or the ABC's in a trauma,
Or a CT,
Or an MRI.

Learn it all.

A Tribute to America's Finest

Zohar Kastner, Grade 11

September 11th, a disastrous day for all the men, women, and children of America. People were fleeing and frantically running as the two tall buildings were tragically falling.

Firemen, police officers, and medical personnel quickly rushed to the horrific scene, but sadly, many of them were never again seen.

When others ran away, they charged forward.
When others ran for safety, they offered their helping hands.
When others cried out for help, they responded with their soothing voices.

Tragically, many of them died. But in doing so, they taught us how to really live. They were heroes, right in front of our very own eyes. They couldn't fly or touch the sky, but they touched others as they sacrificed their lives for them.

On that day, America's finest were revealed—the firefighters, police officers, and medical personnel who gave their lives and struggled to avoid death are now looked upon as America's very best.

Gratitude and thanks are given to all those who helped. And to all those who have perished, we will never forget. Your names will be remembered in the hearts of the American people.

And to all those that have given their lives, we will remember your performances on that horrifying day, and you will be glorified as heroes of America.

Untitled

Bentzy Tanenbaum, Grade 11

Pouring from the sky,
The heavens thundering–
Nowhere you can hide
While bent over in a corner.

Quickly pouring in,
Sweeping everything in sight–
You can't possibly win;
There's no escaping G-d.

Getting in deeper by the minute,
Trying to escape the impossible–
There's no way for the sinner
To leave unharmed.

Crying out for help,
Nothing they could do–
You're left to save yourself
And hope your repentance is accepted.

Jesters

Michael Bernstein, Grade 10

I'd bet my life on the flip of a coin
To walk upon the ivory sand
To dream among the stars and join
The tragic jesters there.

An Unnatural Twilight

Michael Gordon, Grade 11

The alarm buzzed. It sounded distant and indistinct. I opened my eyes and found the world in black and white. The clarity of the picture was bad, too. *Has the new season started already?* I thought. I got out of bed and went to the TV. I found the sharpness knob on the bottom of the screen. It felt soft and fuzzy like everything else, as if the world had been spun around in a cotton candy machine. I turned it and it immediately became more solid under my fingers. The rest of the room came into focus as well. I knew I couldn't do much for the color, so I left that alone.

On my way to the bathroom I passed under an open skylight. I peered up and saw a blackness filled with stars, though it was daylight in the rest of the house. I saw a clock float by and an ethereal door open on cue. I could hear a narrator like a distant droning.

I didn't stay in the bathroom long. I'd been emotionally scarred ever since the electric shaver tried to bite off my lip, the toilet almost swallowed me whole and my toothbrush kept looking at me funny. I checked my reflection to make sure I hadn't been turned into some hideous pig creature. Last season, episode eight left me a little nervous about that.

In the kitchen I found Rod Serling facing a wall and talking to his imaginary audience.

"Joe Nielsen has entered a dimension of sight and sound, shadow and illusion, thought and imagination. A world where old television programs never die, but live on in tedium of despair, where ideas are recycled ad nauseum and commercial breaks are few and far between. He has entered the *Twilight Zone.*" Fade out and cut to commercial. It was just Rod and I for a while.

"Morning, Rod." I went to the mini-bar to mix a drink. I hated when the new season started. It meant every Monday through Friday I had to put up with Rod's introduction and some wacky plot twist every five minutes. I'd broken ten pairs of glasses so far, and all I did was drop them on the floor. Each time the lenses just shattered on contact. *Why does everything break so easily in the Twilight Zone?* I thought. *Honestly!?* "What's on the agenda for today, Rod? Magical stopwatches, phantom chess pieces, evil doppelgangers, savage man-eating sloths? I saved some film from that camera that steals souls. Up for some photography? How about a tape recorder that makes everyone sound like Jimmy Stewart? Have you done that before?"

"Your sarcasm is duly noted, Mr. Nielsen."

I rummaged around in the bar, looking for anything that would take the edge off. When I only found bottles labeled XXX, I remembered that the

60's censors wouldn't allow alcohol on TV. Making the situation worse, my cabinets were all stocked with books marked *To Serve Man, To Serve Duck* and *To Serve Beef.* No breakfast for me today, I guess.

Rod unbuttoned his jacket and sat down in an armchair that seemed to come out of nowhere.

"I'll take a scotch on the rocks, if you've got one." I withdrew two of the XXX bottles and put them on the table. "Sorry, it's all I've got." The façade of stiffness and control drained from Rod's face, leaving only an unhappy artist, trapped within his work. He greedily gulped down some pills with the foul beverage and let the bottle fall to the floor. It shattered into a thousand pieces. Of course.

"I've got it!" Rod exclaimed, "We'll have this drunkard who stumbles upon a beer truck in a post-apocalyptic world and he drops a bottle and... and..."

"Give it up, Rod. You got canned in the 70's; you're not going to make a comeback. And with all due respect, aren't you dead?" He sat for a moment, stunned into silence, but soon began to whimper softly. Shortly he was bawling like a baby. "Oh, come on, Rod. Look, I didn't mean it. You're syndicated on the Sci-Fi channel. That counts for something, right?"

"Oh, for Heaven's sake, who watches the Sci-Fi channel anyway? I'm a disgrace. You don't see Alfred Hitchcock showing up at peoples' houses trying to keep filming. Well, except that one time with Grace Kelly, but he never got past the Monaco secret service. When did my career go down the tube?" He dried his eyes with his tie and collected himself. "It went downhill when we started doing them in color, believe you me. That's when the whole thing just collapsed. That's when I started taking the painkillers. Oh, whom am I kidding? It's all my fault. I should just resign myself to my fate. I'll register for an *E! True Hollywood Story*. I'll pack my things and leave."

Rod was on his way out when I heard a mournful wailing from the closet. I approached the door and found it held in place by a long metal pole. As I stepped closer, I recognized a sound as human. There was someone locked in the closet. I vaguely remembered an episode like this one. I suddenly had a very bad feeling as I pulled away the bar, as if some force of pure diabolical evil were behind it. I heard Rod scream as the stick fell from the lock and the door eased its way open. I peered into the thick darkness and immediately regretted my actions.

It was William Shatner, sitting on a stool with a guitar in his hands, humming to himself. He laughed as he emerged from the shadows, his features changing ever so slightly. Within moments he had transformed himself into "young" William Shatner and disappeared in a shower of low-tech glitter.

I stared at Rod, who had that deer-in-the-headlights look.

"What have you done?"

"Me!? Why do you assume it was me? I didn't do anything. I don't even know how he got there, I swear. Heck, anyone could have let him in; he's very charismatic, you know. I mean, I've never seen him before in my life!"

This could not be tolerated. I'd put up with a lot from Rod over the last couple of seasons, but now he'd gone too far. "You invited a celebrity guest star on. Didn't you?" Rod began to stammer in denial, but I saw through it. "Rod, if you were that desperate for ratings, you should have said something. There's a better way. Come on, we're going to Fox."

Rupert Murdoch's secretary announced our arrival. She was a petite woman, with the usual three fire-breathing heads and barbed teeth of a Fox employee. I suspected nothing wrong, even as she resumed sticking pins in a plush likeness of David Duchovny. A small light blinked on her desk, interrupting her busy needlework. She looked down at the flashing number and said, "Number nine thousand twelve hundred thirty-eight times the fourth root of negative eighteen."

I looked down at the white slip I'd been given. That was our number. I grabbed Rod by the elbow and pulled him towards the door. "Hey, Joe, wait. I think I heard the radical of a negative number in there. Let's be reasonable. I can still leave while I have my dignity."

"Come on, Serling, it's time to enter the big leagues. You need a company like Fox to further your show. And besides, who else is going to hire a monochromatic dead guy?"

"You're right. I'm good enough. I'm smart enough. And doggonitt..."

"Good for you, Rod. Get back on the saddle." He'd definitely gone off the deep end. Thankfully, no one at Fox would notice.

"So, let me get this right, mates," Murdoch queried. "Mr. Serling, you were willing to do anything to keep your show on the air." Rod nodded shamefacedly. "Well, you've come to right place. Just sign on the dotted lines." Murdoch handed Rod a pile of paperwork the size of the James A. Michener/Stephen Hawking joint production – *A Not So Brief History of Everything*. Rod began flipping through it, signing on every dotted, slashed, perforated, underlined and otherwise noted line.

I decided to make small talk with the Undisputed Lord and Master of Fox.

"So, what're you guys at Fox working on nowadays?" Rupert gazed at me with a distracted look on his face. He seemed very interested in the contract Rod was signing.

"Oh, um, well we're working on *Temptation Island II: Sin in Singapore*, *When Animals Attack Survivors* and *Mad Cow TV*." His voice became very distant as Rod got halfway through the paperwork. "Of course, then we'll unveil *Who Wants to Sell Their Soul to be a Millionaire,* and then the final preparations will be complete."

Something Rupert had said disturbed me, but I couldn't quite put my finger on it. *Sin in Singapore* was tacky, but not out of the ordinary for Fox. *When Animals Attack Survivors* was just good healthy competition, and *Mad Cow TV* was just matching *Saturday Night Liver Cancer.* Then it hit me.

I tried to pull the papers away from Rod, but everything moved in slow motion. He was on the last page of the Devil's Contract. Literally. I saw the pen scrape along the page with agonizing slowness, but I could do nothing.

R...o...d... "You've finally figured it out," Rupert chuckled, sharp fangs emerging from his mouth. His voice echoed in my head like a telepathic hissing and Rod was totally oblivious. "Your friend is signing away his afterlife, and there's nothing you can do."

S...e... "His immortal soul will belong to me. He'll spend all eternity writing bad *Tales from the Crypt* rip-offs. But don't worry, maybe I'll allow him a contract renegotiation...in about thirty millennia." He laughed maniacally. The transformation from horrifying geriatric Australian business tycoon to slightly less horrifying demonic being of absolute Evil was complete. Oddly, it didn't take long.

r...l...i... "You can save on airfare, hotels, cabs, warp-drives and plasma emitters." The disembodied voice of William Shatner floated through my subconscious. "Priceline.com. Prrriiiiiccceeeliiiiiiine doooootttt cooooooom. Thank you and goodnight." Finally I screamed, but it was too late.

g.

"It is complete. Rod Serling's soul now belongs to Fox Broadcasting, a division of Fox Searchlight, a division of 20th Century Fox, a division of Satanica Inc. All rights and privileges of said soul belong to me. Further legal work will be handled by the law firm of Mephistopheles, Beelzebub, Lucifer, Hades, and Starr. Come along now, Mr. Serling."

"No, you can't take him." This wasn't my business. I shouldn't have gotten involved. But I couldn't stand idly by and watch someone get drafted into eternal indenture to Fox. "We'll get another lawyer to dispute this contract. You'll be in court for the next ten eons."

Rupert/Satan merely laughed. "FOOL! Where on Earth are you going to find a lawyer not already employed by the Devil. Passing the bar requires a standard de-souling everywhere except Los Angeles and D.C., and anyone living there has already sold his soul." He had me there. "There's nowhere to go. I control the law, the afterlife and the media. All non-infernal networks, radio stations, websites and publishers have been eliminated. The masses belong to me."

Hellfire ascended from a pit in the floor of the office. From within the flames stepped out Regis Philbin, Jeff Probst, Anne Robinson, the cast of *7th Heaven*, the entire WWF, and various other celebrities. "Do you see now that you cannot fight me? Even Regis, the lovable King of TV, was taken over to the Dark Side." A lawyer briefly appeared and stated that "Dark Side" is registered trademark of Lucas films and is reproduced with permission. Suddenly a burst of inspiration gave me a plan.

"You think you've won, Satan? Well, I know of one individual who would never bow down to you and your malevolent machinations, mainly because he's too preoccupied with his own and worships no god other than himself." I withdrew from my pocket the magical remote control from *Twilight Zone* season twenty, episode nineteen. I aimed at the wall and clicked. At first there was nothing but static. Then an image appeared. It was PBS. One of those annoying film buffs was interviewing George Lucas. I reached into the wall and pull the bearded "master of science fiction" out of public broadcast television and into the deeper regions of Hell.

I didn't need to explain anything to George; he was already in action. He withdrew his double edged light-saber and began hacking celebrities to bits. He was midway through the cybernetic components of the robotic Anne Robinson, or maybe that was just the regular Anne Robinson, when Rupert's minions attacked him from behind.

"Lucas Films is no longer the last bastion against my empire. I have already taken many of your closest and dearest. Yoda has been granted his life-long dream of playing Ms. Piggy's love interest in *The Muppets Go to the Betty Ford Clinic*. Samuel L. Jackson has agreed to sign on to do movies for us...where his character will actually have a name and more than five nanoseconds worth of dialogue. We have even taken Jake 'Little Vader' Lloyd hostage and will soon begin combining his DNA with that of Haley Joel Osment to create the perfect child star. Give up, Lucas, there's nothing left." George wailed in sorrow. All seemed to be lost.

"Take him down to the room we have prepared for him in the Francis Ford Coppola wing," Murdoch/Lucifer said, "and show him the punishment for creating good sequels." They began dragging George into the pit of fire. I knew I had to do something. I sidled up behind Rupert and whispered in his ear. He smiled and nodded.

"Oh yes, and George, I am your father." That did it. *Spaceballs* had been one thing, the 80's had been full of *Star Wars* parodies, but now he'd had enough. No one overused classic Lucas clichés without paying the price. George threw off the evil creatures that held him and stalked toward Murdoch. 'You've gone too far now, trash-trafficker. Mmm, that's an idea, a garbage freighter from the planet Down-under-ine with an inexplicably Australian accent. Now, prepare to be Jedi-capitated."

Well, George didn't fare so well once the WWF writers finished scripting the choreography for the wrestlers. After what happened to his face, I don't think George is going to smell what anyone's cooking. As for Rod and me, we ended up in the pit of never-ending black and white sitcoms. So nothing much has changed. I'm told the war for world domination still wages on, but that no longer interests me. Who cares if Rupert Murdoch rules Earth? All I'm concerned with is how Lucy's going to get into Ricky's show at the Club Copa Mambo Cabana Chickita Babbaloo without having some 'splaining to do.

The End

Anteroom

Michael Bernstein, Grade 10

I'm standing at the gates of death
And wondering what to say.
The devil's taken full control,
My angel's gone away.
The whole world has forsaken me
And now I'll have to pay,
For they see things in black and white
While I see things in gray.

The answer's in the question's making
Even though the asker's faking.
I'd give out help, but no one's taking,
And even now, my soul is shaking.

I'm stepping up the ivory stairs
And wondering what to do.
There you are in all your glory,
And I can't get past you.
You have placed the fate of many
In the vengeful hand of few,
For other children you have spared
But all firstborn you slew.

Below me, twisted dawn is breaking
And now the dew-damp ground is baking.
On my bare feet, the mud is caking.
By now, the master's hand is aching.

I'm running out of death's back door,
So drained and battle-worn.
Black-and-white prophets need me
Because gray-sight in the morn
Decides if someone's thread of life
Will hold, or will be torn.
But even dead can die,
And I am one of the firstborn.

Around my ankles, mist is snaking,
Sent by Night-Queen, thinned by Day-King.
And, finally, my angel's waking,
But, still, my tortured soul is shaking.

The devil takes the sun's red eye
And casts it on the marble floor.
The heat of flaming indecision
Chills me to the core.
Angel now retreats in fright
And, blocks the way to Elysium shore.
Escape is now impossible.
I'm shaking even more.

The answer's in the question's making
Even though the asker's faking.
I'd give out help, but no one's taking.
Anteroom, my soul is shaking.

Night

Benjy Berman, Grade 9

Darkness of night drowns out the light,
And the romance, however absent, roams free.
Silence and love is what it covets,
And the moon hangs on it like a dove in a tree.
Night is enigmatic uncertainty, a time
When the sad turn happy, and the shy turn sly.
Night is a shadowy cupid striking
Its people with life and love.
People become what they are not.
Night smiles and never frowns.
Dreams are the water where one drowns.
For night is what no one thinks,
And, if inside, if you fall, you shall smile.

A Tragic Account

Neal Davis, Grade 11

It was the average day in the life of a New Yorker. Subways were running the normal route. People were traveling the same way they did every day, until it hit. It bewildered everyone. It was not expected at all—the terrorist attack on the United States, beginning with a hijacked plane hitting the first tower of the World Trade Center. Then a second hijacked plane crashed into the second tower, followed by the attack on the Pentagon. It filled the world with anxiety and suspense, wondering the extent of the terrorists' abilities.

The media started screaming the headline, "America Under Attack." Manhattan was secluded. Many were without jobs. Others were trapped within the city; there was no way of getting home. Some people were not able to reach their spouses or relatives to tell them they were safe. The gruesome acts of terror left everyone in fear of the unknown and the unexpected. Many people have left us. Some of them became heroes in their attempts to save others.

Emergency and rescue squads rushed to the scene, cleaning up the wreckage and trying to find bodies buried within. Their efforts were not so fruitful. Few of the number of missing were accounted for; the rest are still buried or unfound.

Lazy Afternoon on the Interstate

Michael Bernstien, Grade 10

Above my head
The sky is dead
Where clouds fly by
As if to spy
On me.
Under my feet
Lies a dead street
As cars drive fast
(and quickly) past
Occasionally.

Human Truth

Bentzy Tanenbaum, Grade 11

The mystery of this world
No one will ever know.
Don't ask any questions
'Cause there is no answer.

They say this is the way,
But I know that couldn't be.
I approach and ask them why,
And they just make up excuses.

The more you deny
The further you get from human truth.

Life and its abnormality,
Impossible to understand.
We had better stick to reality
'Cause nothing happens without reason.

Not everything is explainable
Even though it may seem so to some.
It just gets them into more trouble
As they go along with their lives.

Things don't suddenly happen.
The truth is just hidden from our eyes.
Only One knows the real reason
Even though it does not seem justified.

Night

Michael Levine, Grade 9

What be the night?
Night is secrecy, the freedom to wish.
It is a wish, a hope for the future,
A time of healing and peace, for restoring the soul.
Night is like drunkenness, time for irrational dreams.
What be the night?
The night contains all.

Revolution

Sam Flaks, Grade 12

Revolution! Waiter! Each of these words is customarily shouted with the desperate urgency of unsatisfied demand. Welded together, a dissonant sounding and absurd "Waiters' Revolution" is produced. I can attest to the existence of the very real, if very microscopic, Waiters' Revolution at a summer camp nestled in the Catskills. At the beginning of camp, waiters were prepared to do a reasonably competent job. I was clumsy but very solicitous to my young, cute "customers."

Soon, however, our discontent grew. Reasonable men asked (and will ask again), "Why can't the waiters get leave on days the whole camp is out on a trip?" Furthermore, we were starved for the adrenaline rush that only a competitive camp sports league can provide. Objectively, we were 15-year-olds whiling and whining away our vacation relaxing, spiced by light work in the dining room. Subjectively, we were oppressed and disrespected, second-class citizens compared to the privileged junior counselors who were our peers. Tension grew ever more pervasive in the teapot, bubbling and frothing from the sides.

The kettle cracked on a Jewish fast day, traditionally a day for moaning and complaining. We were all hungry and tired and should not have been required to serve others before we revived ourselves. All the waiters planned to refuse to serve the meal that would break the fast, dooming the rest of the camp to a 15-minute delay before eating. Of course, we waiters would immediately take food for ourselves. We calculated (correctly as it turned out) that we would not be punished. As the hour approached, I felt the stirrings of a cruel dilemma: to join my friends in cozy solidarity with a cause grounded in fairness but pursued selfishly and myopically, or to cross the picket line and defect to an unfair authority for the service of the greater good. I had a change of heart and pleaded with the other waiters not to delay the meal, but it was to no avail. As pandemonium descended upon the dining hall, I was caught in the crossfire between irate counselors and steadfast waiters. Emerging from a protective, irresolute crouch, I straightened my back and assumed an upright posture. I crossed the Rubicon, cast the die, and went to Canossa. In sum, I served the meal.

An over-dramatic but idealistic clash of facets of my personality made it inevitable that I would play a part in fomenting the Waiters' Revolution, but it also dictated my defection when the situation disintegrated into a capricious disregard of the greater good. I had welcomed the opportunity to rebel against authority when the stakes seemed so low. Unexpectedly, young children became the victims of our quarrels with the administration and were deprived of food longer than necessary after a long fast.

I still feel guilty for double-crossing the Waiters. I knew my colleagues were a generally mellow bunch who had been stirred to action based on a sense of injustice – one which I shared. On one hand, an extra half hour spent serving the camp first seemed noble. On the other, I had been raised to root for the underdog. When the counselors of the youngest bunks subsequently thanked me for helping out, it only made me feel worse. I did not want to benefit, but, nevertheless, I did.

Throughout the whole episode, from my first complaints to my last reluctant decision, I was driven by an inordinate appetite for personal grandeur, and I exaggerated small events to infuse them with great meaning. I suspect both my initial escapist talk about a "strike" and then my serious admonishments to serve the meal had an equally negligible effect on my disenchanted colleagues.

In the final analysis, I was a pretty clumsy waiter.

Out of the Ordinary

Shimon Rosenbaum, Grade 12

Weird, different, quiet and slow,
Don't be afraid of people you don't know.
A person with disabilities is no different from you and me,
So why can't society just let them be?
Everybody wants to wear cargo pants and be the same.
If you dress or act differently, people think you're insane.
People who want to be different and make a stand
Seem to be ignored and always banned.
When you see someone who's different walking down the street,
Don't run away and shuffle you're feet.
Individuals are unique with their point of view,
And their philosophy is, "You should be unique, too."
There's no denying it. The facts don't vary.
Individuals are looked upon as "out of the ordinary."

Entertainment

Michael Bernstein, Grade 10

Life is a movie,
A Hollywood sleeper
With cool background music
Like "Don't Fear the Reaper,"
Which plays at the end
When the hero dies
While the heroine sits
By the bed and cries.

Life is a one-act,
Off-Broadway play.
The critics all love it.
Onstage it'll stay.
Its run's been extended,
Its budget, too.
But the actors will die soon,
And so will the crew.

Cool

Bentzy Tanenbaum, Grade 11

You think because you change, you look cool.
You think because you change, you are different.
But I know the truth about you inside;
You are nothing other than the previous.

Trying to be something other than what you are,
You think that will make you better.
In life you are small but trying to appear large.
No one is being fooled but yourself.

To everyone your antics are just a show and tell,
Deciding to show others what you're not.
All these fake actions are just an outer shell;
When split open, you are as destitute as before.

Chanukah

Moshe Kamioner, Grade 9

As the eighth night passes by,
We light the candles on the menorah.
Now the spirit of Chanukah will die,
But never the flame of the Torah.

In school the next morning,
We light them one more time.
We find the lights to be adorning,
And we give the *pushka* a dime.

The fire flares in our heart,
And we savor every last moment.
For G-d's wonderful and amazing art
Relieves our soul of torment.

As the wax begins to melt,
The candle quickly shrinks.
A sense of warmth is felt,
Strengthening our ancient links.

Each candle stops its burn,
Each at its own separate time,
The season begins to turn,
And so ends this rhyme.

Feel Pain for the Messiah

Anonymous

The time has come for the ascension to the heights
There have been too many long and bloody nights
The suffering has gone on long enough
Our enemies are getting strong and tough
The time has come for the ascension to the heights

The end is near for our pathetic minds
We soon will sever the last tie that binds
The prejudice has escalated fast
But all of us keep fighting 'til the last
The end is near for our pathetic minds

Metaphysical tingles run up and down my spine
The starting gun begets the finish line
The clichés follow me as my head spins
I try to explain life, as black death wins,
The time has come for the ascension to the heights.

Dark Strife

Moshe Frances, Grade 12

Darkness falls upon the sky.
Where hast thou gone through the night?

"Who are you and what do you want?"
He replied, "Do you know me and what I'm about?"

A scream so harsh it's not hard out figure out.
I cause suffering without a doubt.
Those who are weak will strike out!

Unsung Sonnet

Michael Goon, Grade 11

I entreat forgiveness; I broke your heart.
Little flame of passion my match had lit,
Beckoned close to sit, then extinguished it.
Blossom vividly painted; fruit so tart,
Playing my loud music, sauntering so smart,
Empty of emotion, my heart lacked wit.
Love you in heart, if not mind did permit.
Mind's eye's constant gaze, did conscience yet thwart?
Soul did elsewhere roam, to follow Path
For us did I learn: Truth complements Life.
You were, for me, special… Him, holy.
To mar beauty in, for beauty out, Wrath.
To cut flower from Source to scent it, Strife.
To see only my footprints on the Path, Folly.

A Litvak

Shimshon Ayzenberg, Grade 11

A heavy snowstorm engulfed a gloomy dawn and whitened the northern *shtetl.* Waves of biting wind left delicate designs on the windows and slippery ice on dusty aisles. As roosters voiced their vexing melodies in farms throughout, three bearded "early birds" clothed in thick hides, *straimalach,* leather galoshes, and fluffy mittens, slowly roamed across the snowy ocean and desolate fields towards the pond.

They carefully approached the middle of the pond and cracked open a hole within to proceed with the dipping ritual. To cleanse themselves from the sticky sins and the evil urge of *sitra achra*, each dipped three times in the frosty water. Then, suddenly, they saw the figure of a man in the distance. Instantly the three, feeling their heartbeats, gazed until the man's form became fully discernable.

A Litvak appeared. He was extremely exhausted and thus fell, indenting his frigid body into the thick layers of snow. The three bearded men escorted him back to the *shtetl* and placed multiple blankets on him, for they could not afford wood or fire. After his full recovery, the Litvak admitted that the heavy snowstorm caused him to stray from his preplanned hike and that *hashkho protas* brought him to the *shtetl.*

The next day, the entire community of the northern *shtetl* congregated to chant the morning prayers. It was a very peculiar prayer in comparison to what the Litvak was accustomed to, but what really puzzled him was the absence of the Rebbe. In addition, there was no other sanctuary within hundreds of kilometers.

"How could the Rebbe," the Litvak pondered, "supposedly a man of faith, excuse himself from the compelling prayers to G-d?" The Rebbe didn't appear the next morning and the many mornings after that. The Litvak grew increasingly agitated and doubtful of the holy teaching of the *Besht.* "The Rebbe is a fool," the Litvak vehemently hollered in old Yiddish.

One early morning, determined to expose the Rebbe, the Litvak followed him through the frosty woods, past white cottages, and into the dusky grove near a frozen prairie. There, he witnessed the Rebbe cutting down trees and carrying the logs to a decrepit cottage nearby. Then, gazing through the icy windows of the cottage, the Litvak observed the Rebbe making fire, boiling water, and preparing tea. Next to the Rebbe, he noticed an elderly *Yid* sitting on a dusty couch. The *Yid*'s face was glowing and so was the Rebbe's. But the Litvak's was not. On the contrary, he gazed in sadness and horror at the elderly *Yid*'s missing legs.

Friendships

Moshe Kanarfogel, Grade 10

All kinds of friends, old and new,
Plain friends and best friends, school friends too.
Which are most important, which come first?
Which do you like the best, which are the worst?

Do you like your school friends and think they're cool?
Or are they only your friends because they're in school?
Do you consider them close, like a sister or brother?
Or once you go home, you don't know each other?

Are best friends real, or are they also fake?
Do you return their favors, or do you just take?
Are any of your best friends important, special, and vital?
Or are you only best friends just for the title?

What about plain friends, are they just the same?
Do you really like the person, or just know his name?
Is a friend the starting point, like a deep-rooted stem?
Or are you nice because you don't want to hurt him?

When thinking about this, your mind and heart fight
Until they realize that neither is right.
A friend can last longer because you fight less.
A best friend you talk to more, a difficult test.

Nobody can tell you whom you should like.
Nobody can tell you which memories to strike.
Friends can be difficult, as it's been shown.
But, friends are important; without them you're alone.

Last Story

Jeremy Bleiberg, Grade 11

Crossing through my garden,
Walking out the door,
Father, I beg pardon,
I can't take it anymore.

I keep dwelling upon the past,
That one final mistake,
Sinking down all too fast,
Heart straining toward a break.

In one moment I lost her,
In two I was in tears.
I said I'd always love her,
Won't give in to her fears.

But then she turned and walked away,
Leaving me to stare.
I swear I won't forget that day.
She didn't even care.

Now that's my story, Father,
That's why I've got to burn.
Can't stop me, please don't bother.
I'll be gone when you return.

I'm tired of those echoes
That whisper in my head.
That's how my last story goes;
It's over when I'm dead.

The Death of JFK

Zach Kornhauser, Grade 10

A hot windy day in late November,
This is the day they all remember.
The day they opened the graveyard gates
For the most respected man in the United States.
In that most turbulant southern state,
The President sat there like free bait;
President John F. Kennedy, to be exact,
A Democratic president as a matter of fact.

Now the President sat helplessly there,
For, in his mind, he had no fear.
He grandly rode through the town,
With a smile and not a frown.
Soon the driver could barely steer;
In his head there was great fear.

The driver's fear was not absurd,
The President's cries were later heard.
The sniper, hidden to some degree,
Wanted to cause great tragedy.
He looked through his sniper scope,
His lips sealed like an envelope.
The rifle fired with a thud!
From the President's head a trail of blood.

Lee Harvey Oswald was the accused,
As police searched for the gun he used.
Kennedy died a hero, the papers read.
One of the greatest presidents is dead.

9/11/01

Max Wein, Grade 12

On September 11, 2001,
The entire American nation became united.
Democrats, Republicans, Liberals, Conservatives,
It didn't matter.
We were all Americans.
The Twin Towers didn't represent a political party,
Neither did the Pentagon.
Both represented America.
The firemen and police officers who perished while saving others
Represented America.
The military that is currently defending our freedom
Represents America.
There are no more Blacks, Whites, Chinese, Hispanics,
Russians, Israelis, etc.
Only Americans.
GOD BLESS AMERICA

Requirements for Bliss

Moshe Schiffmiller, Grade 10

Comfort
Safety
Warmth
Coziness
Relaxation
Adoration
Longing
Satiation
Sensitivity
Caring
Silence
Time Stands Still

Me

Yaakov Kay, Grade 10

I sit in my room, in front of my computer,
Searching my thoughts for ideas that will suit her.
I wonder aloud if my teacher will realize
That an assignment such as this is what I despise.
Mathematics and science come easier to me,
A doctor or engineer is what I'm likely to be.
Writing means reading, and reading's no fun.
I'd rather watch TV or be out in the sun.

Sports, such as hockey, give me much enjoyment,
Cross checks and wrist shots – I'm good at deployment.
This is not to say my brain I don't exercise,
In *Gemara Shiur* I often will energize.

And now a few words about my physical appearance:
I'm told I'm a combination of both my parents.
I'm thankful I'll likely be as tall as my dad,
And I have wavy brown hair like he had as a lad.
My mom's dark brown eyes and very straight nose
Are apparent on my face as I strike up a pose.
Last, but not least, I'm a student at best,
So I will now take my leave and go to bed for some rest.

Respect

Max Wein, Grade 12

If you're not going to respect the people who gave you life,
Whom will you respect?
If you're not going to respect the people who changed you daily,
Whom will you respect?
If you're not going to respect the people who stayed up all night because of your cries,
Whom will you respect?
If you're not going to respect the people who took care of you when you were sick,
Whom will you respect?
If you're not going to respect the people who paid a fortune for your education,
Whom will you respect?
If you're not going to respect the people who will always love you, no matter what,
Whom will you respect?
If you're not going to respect your parents,
Whom will you respect?

Mirror

Elan Nyer, Grade 10

Many people think the mirror is the finest invention.
What could be better? A device that lets you make
Sure you got your external appearance to perfection.

All that mirrors do is make people vain,
And they seem to drive people insane.

Why should a mirror show you if you're skinnier or fatter?
Shouldn't it show you what really matters?

Shouldn't a mirror show what's inside?
Isn't that your one feature you shouldn't hide?

My Grandfather

Yehudah Rosenblatt, Grade 9

How many lads have a grandpa like mine?
So jolly and cheerful, anywhere he'll shine.
His great smile shows all the love in his heart,
Not to mention all of his great smarts.
He's an avid reader, reading book after book.
He leaves it to his wife to be a great cook.

Cooking, baking, what a chef she is,
Satisfying that great hunger of his.
He likes her roast beef and potatoes too,
And ask for seconds is what he'll do.

My grandpa is truly the best,
Careful to make a kind gest,
He's always there in the clutch,
And that's why I love him so much.

Two Perspectives: The Vagabond and The Sailor

Yaakov Meir Nemoy, Grade 12

See that man on those boxes.
Watching him work, the children stand,
Fascinated. He tells stories of adventure,
Treasure, and pirates. From their windows,
The girls look, wondering who'll be the lucky lady.

All they see are bronzed muscles and amazing stories,
And don't know the danger of life. My skin, pale
In comparison, and my frame, small, cannot compete.
I know only the fear of pursuit and the pain of friends
Betrayed and lost to the cause and the freedom of the sea.
But it is not for me; I get seasick easily.

See that man at the bar.
Watching him recount, the girls listen,
Fascinated. He tells stories of adventure,
Loot, and thieves. Upstairs,
The girls look, wondering who'll be the lucky lady.

All they see is a thoughtful mind and amazing stories
And don't know the danger of life. My mind, simple
In comparison, and my large body, clumsy, cannot compete.
I know only the fear of storms and the pain of friends
Lost to the sea and storms and the freedom of anarchy.
But it is not for me; I am too noisy.

Calls of the Wild

Chayim Goldberg, Grade 11

The rustling of leaves
The gurgling of streams
The howling of wolves
The growling of bears
The hooting of owls
The chirping of crickets
The sound of blowing wind–
These are my calls.
My calls to the woods,
My calls to the forest,
My calls to my home.
These are my calls to the wild.

Cloudy Night

Yaakov Meir Nemoy, Grade 12

Spotted and blue hue
Full lit moon, awe and beauty,
And I stare for hours.

The Joy of Comic Strips
or
Popular Culture in Three Easy Panels: A Look into the World of Comic Strips and Their Ties to 90's Culture

Michael Gordon, Grade 12

All forms of popular culture, be they TV, movies, magazines, or any other medium, are not created in a vacuum. Entertainers and their creations are deeply shaped by that which is happening in the world around them. Furthermore, these media can have far-reaching effects on the culture in which they exist. The 1990's were a decade of rapid technological progress and commercial revolution. The birth of the "information age" changed nearly every aspect of the lives of individuals, companies and even nations. The exponential increase in computer use, the popularity of the Internet, and the new interconnectedness of the global community all profoundly affected the domestic, business and political cultures of the 90's.

Many forms of entertainment and diversion are affected by cultural trends, but few reflect society's "Zeitgeist" as much as comics, caricatures and political cartoons. The very fact that most people obtain their regular intake of comics while reading the newspaper, their constant source of daily pertinent information, indicates how linked comic strips are to the way we view our world. Furthermore, the typical newspaper is not limited to comics of a particular genre or focus; the funny pages are filled with diverse forms of humor, from the sarcastic irony of *Doonesbury* to ingenuous schoolyard fun of *Peanuts* to the bizarre abstract humor of Gary Larson's *Farside*, each appealing to a different segment or mindset of the population.

The medium of cartoons always has had an important role in American culture. In the late 1800's, political cartoons served the nation with a humorous bent on our socio-politico-economic woes. At that time in history, society was turning its focus inward on the growing corruption in the government. For the 1990's, however, the corporate world became the center of public attention, with one particular voice at the forefront.

Dilbert, initially created by Scott Adams as a way to amuse his coworkers at Pacific Bell, was introduced to the public in 1989 and subsequently amassed great popularity in the newborn Nineties. Originally a themeless hodgepodge of puns and punch lines, starring an underdog named Dilbert and his power-hungry pet, Adams's strip found its calling in workplace humor. By the mid-nineties, *Dilbert*, syndicated worldwide in over a thousand newspapers and used by dozens of companies and organizations as a sure-fire marketing tool, was already being hailed as the voice of the cubicle-confined, manager-plagued, white-collar worker. Using ideas familiar to himself and anyone else who had been forced to work in 90's corporate America, Scott Adams expressed the pent-up frustration of millions of office workers in the United States as well as the rest of the world. But what brought about this new focus on the business world?

Since the end of the 1950's, the American family unit has been in a constant state of decay. In popular culture, too, the strength of the nuclear family has been fading. Increasingly television has been replacing home-oriented shows with either "buddy" shows, such as *Seinfeld* or *Friends*, or workplace situations. By the end of the twentieth century, however, the emphasis was almost entirely removed from the family and placed partly on the shoulders of the business unit, as seen in shows like *ER, The Drew Carey Show* or *Spin City*.[1]

The major themes of *Dilbert* relate mostly to the plight of workers under evil and/or clueless bosses. Despite many seemingly far-out exaggerations of the typical employee struggle, Scott Adams still seems to be accurately reflecting the experiences of workers everywhere. Adams, in an introduction to his book *The Dilbert Principle*, writes:

> "Most of the themes in my comic strip *Dilbert* involve workplace situations. I routinely include bizarre and unworldly elements such as sadistic talking animals, troll-like accountants, and employees turning into dishrags after the life-force has been drained from their bodies. And yet the comment I hear most often is:
>
> 'That's just like my company.'
>
> No matter how absurd I try to make the comic strip I can't stay ahead of what people are experiencing in their own workplaces."[2]

Even more amazing are the thousands of e-mails Adams receives, which describe true tales of office sadism or incompetence that are the real life equivalents to all that happens in Dilbert's world.

The reason why the business world is so fraught with these types of situations, according to Adams, is in part due to the constant technological revolutions that defined the 90's. The fact that Dilbert and his colleagues are engineers is no arbitrary detail. Adams chose engineers as his main characters, though he himself has never been an engineer, presumably because of their connection to technology. The proliferation of computer use, the veneration of the Internet and the globalization of the economy all had unique effects from the engineering standpoint.

On more than one occasion Dilbert has been accosted, degraded or replaced by a robot, android or apparatus of his own creation. The idea of our own inventions becoming greater than us has been around since the beginnings of the Industrial Revolution. To some it would now seem that the same fear that blue-collar workers had of machines and assembly lines is encroaching on the white-collar world in the form of increasingly faster computers. Though the idea of machines replacing man is purely science fiction – for the moment – there is a palpable dehumanization of the skilled workforce. Coupled with ever-present greed, this attitude towards employees has had profound effects on the 90's. In a review of Adams's second book, *Dogbert's Top Secret Management Handbook*, *Entertainment Weekly* staff writer Lisa Schwarzbaum writes,

> "Boiling all of human existence down to the relationship between management and workers reduces contemporary life to its psychological essence. 'This isn't the "me" generation of the eighties,' Dilbert's boss warns an overworked, outspoken underling in one comic strip… 'This is the "lifeless nineties."'"[3]

The devaluing of human equality in the workplace, in stark contrast to the increasing feeling of personal freedom developing around the world during the modern era, created a scenario of unrest seething beneath the surface of the business world.

Without a doubt, Scott Adams's most prevalent theme is the overwhelming stupidity that plagues our modern world. He writes at length about it in *The Dilbert Principle* and, despite a total lack of scientific proof (after all, according to empirical studies the average I.Q. is getting higher), makes a persuasive argument for the general incompetence of the human race:

> "I proudly include myself in the idiot category. Idiocy in the modern age isn't an all-encompassing, twenty-four hour situation for most people. It's a condition that everybody slips into many times a day. Life is just too complicated to be smart all the time."[4]

That is the thesis of *Dilbert*. Science, politics, economics, and other social sciences have become so complex that we can't realistically be expected to be fully aware or productive all the time. As a result of our growing idiocy relative to the complexities of our world, we are forced to make random, uninformed decisions in the hopes that something inadvertently goes our way.[4] The 90's were a perfect time for applied arbitrariness. Americans were facing monolithic competition from Japan and impoverished Asian countries in the areas of technology and cheap goods production, respectively. America also had the disadvantage of stricter regulations on employers as well as differences of attitude, and many companies were forced to rely simply on chance and luck to get them through these hard times.

One of *Dilbert*'s, and Scott Adams's, most ardent critics is Norman Solomon, author of "Media Beat," a popular syndicated column on media and politics. Solomon claims that Adams is, in reality, no friend of the troubled worker, but is really a lackey to corporate executives. According to Solomon, people think that within the humor of *Dilbert*, Adams is "laughing with them. But is he actually laughing at them?"[5] Further, Solomon asserts that *Dilbert* is meant to prevent workers form realizing their plight and seeking out better conditions for themselves. To Norman Solomon this comic strip that has defined business for the 90's is Marx's "opiate of the masses" and deleterious to the cause of the workers.

For the record, Scott Adams has yet to give a formal response to Solomon's accusations. He has made reference in his later books to many of the criticisms made against him, but it is impossible to prove either Adams or Solomon as the victor in their indirect skirmish. However, it is clear that *Dilbert* has had an overwhelming impact on the past decade. Whether it provides workers with a temporary diversion from dealing with the trials and tribulations caused by stupidity (which, using Adams's thesis, is not likely to disappear, so long as humans remain humans), or subverts their desire for better treatment, or simply helps us all put a face on the struggling climate of our economic situation, *Dilbert* has had obvious, as well as still unseen, repercussions across all sectors of the business world.[6]

Notes

[1]Lisa Schwarzbaum, "Comic-Strip Relief," *Entertainment Weekly Book Review.* http://www.ew.com/r0/ew/Search_Links_Clk/in?/ew/archive/0,1798,1|19879|0|dilbert,00.html

[2]Scott Adams, *The Dilbert Principle.* (United States of America, Harper Collins Publishing, 1996), 1.

[3]Ibid, 3.

[4]Scott Adams, *Random Acts of Management.* (United States of America: United Features Syndicate Inc., 2000), 7.

[5]Norman Solomon, *Excerpt from: the Trouble with Dilbert.* http://free.freespeech.org/normansolomon/dilbert/book/1.html

[6]Alexandra Jacobs, *"Dilbert" Deliberation.* http://www.ew.com/r0/ew/Search_Links_Clk/in?/ew/archive/0,1798,1|22330|0|dilbert,00.html

Ode to My Sister

Shimon Rosenbaum, Grade 12

The people who know her call her Dee,
And she's the greatest sister there will ever be.
Her eyes are a beautiful green; her hair is straight and black.
She's the sweetest person; she'll always cut me slack.
She plays her guitar while sitting on her bed,
Songs from the Stones and the Grateful Dead.
She sits and talks to me when my eyes are full of tears.
She explains the world to me, all her anxieties and fears.
She's not only fun, but also extremely smart.
Most of all, Dee has a warm heart.
I love my sister – she's my true hero,
Always making me feel like a hundred, never a zero.

Maniacal Adage

Michael Bernstein, Grade 10

I say things that might seem inane
But only because I am insane.
Everybody thinks I am lazy.
(They're wrong; I'm only slightly crazy.)
They put me in the honor's track
Although I am a maniac.
I can't see why it's *I* they'd pick.
Can't they see I'm a lunatic?!

The explanation's not high-tech.
It's really not that long:
I *am* playing with a full deck,
But the cards are shuffled wrong.

Talent

A poem of ego, frustration and unrealized potential.

Michael Gordon, Grade 12

'Tis a waste that I can write.
'Tis a waste that I can think.
For what purpose do they serve
If thought does not meet ink?

Though of these two faculties
I have an excess of my fair share,
I cannot seem to make them work
As one productive pair.

Some dozen years I've had the gift
For writing words and verse;
Yet not one single story written
For better or for worse.

A thousand tales and fancies
Pile up upon my brain.
My pen spews forth artistry,
But for grades, and thus, in vain.

What an irony it is,
A cruelty of the Divine,
To waste such skill and acumen
On a wretched soul as mine.

Hated Darkness

Jeremy Bleiberg, Grade 11

Sitting in this living hell,
Confined to life like a prison cell,
Left to my thoughts like a g-d scorned,
Friends and family, they never mourned.
Feeling has left me; my body's gone numb,
Lost in the darkness as if deaf, blind, and dumb,
Submitting to pain to stay in the game,
My love's long been gone, yet I'm still the same.
The walls of my cell start to cave in,
But I'm ready now. Let it begin.

The Language Barrier

Moshe Schiffmiller, Grade 10

It stops you from communicating with your neighbor,
From understanding a historical document,
From negotiating.

It hurts the world every moment,
Sabotaging friendly efforts,
Causing chaos and anarchy.

When will it end?
When we all pick a common language,
Or when we learn to speak every existing one?

Hopefully never.
Difference in language is important;
Our heritage and individuality come from it.

It has a bad reputation.
But give it a chance–
The future could be worse than the present.

The Great Beyond

Shimon Rosenbaum, Grade 12 &
Mayer Kadoch, Grade 12

A world of wonder up above,
White specks scattered like salt,
A beautiful vision like a floating dove,
In this wondrous place you'll find no fault.

You look at it through a telescope;
You see all different shapes.
That's where you figure out your horoscope,
Either your impending doom or joyous fate.

You probably know what it is by now.
If you don't, we'll tell you just in case.
Looking at it will make you say, "How?"
This glorious world is none other than space.

The Holocaust

Ari Weber, Grade 9

The Holocaust was a black time in our history as Jews. It is so horrible to hear the stories from survivors and read of their harrowing accounts in books. Consider how horrible it was to experience it first-hand.

My *Zaidy*, Reb Mair Weber, a survivor from the labor camps, tells the following story.

The year was 1945 in Veruchta, Poland. *Zaidy* was a 20-year-old yeshiva *bochur* who had been studying under the supervision of the Rav for *Smicha*. He was taken from his yeshiva along with the entire student body to a labor camp, where they were forced to clear land mines, chop down trees, and rebuild roads for the advancing German army. They endured many hardships such as malnutrition, torture, and exhaustion. They worked long hours, walked for days without sleep, and wore only a thin layer of clothing that didn't protect them from the cold. Fatigued, many fell where they stood and either died or were killed right then and there.

My *Zaidy* had a good friend named Yossi Weiss, who lived with him through all this. One day, Yossi decided to try to escape because he had had "enough." Yossi had heard in the distance the sounds of Russian guns and canon fire and wanted to join the Russian army. The German soldier in charge thought that *Zaidy* and Yossi were Russian spies and that Yossi had left in order to pass along information. *Zaidy* knew nothing about Yossi's whereabouts. (Many assumed he was killed by a land mine because no one heard from him after that.) Nevertheless, the Germans detained and tortured my *Zaidy* for two days in the barracks because they thought they could get information out of him. *Zaidy* kept professing his innocence and said he knew nothing about Yossi.

Finally, a German soldier put *Zaidy* in a box with a rope around his neck intending to hang him. At that moment, *Zaidy* said, "I'll tell you whatever you want to hear, but the truth is, I don't know where he is." With the rope around his neck and the German soldier ready to hang him, he saw in the distance an SS soldier on horseback racing towards him, and simultaneously saw the Spinka Rav before his eyes saying, "Don't worry, everything is going to be okay – nobody will hurt you." Right after that, the SS soldier told the other German soldier to cut him loose immediately. The SS soldier and the Spinka Rav then disappeared at that moment.

It is apparent to anyone who believes in miracles that the *Yad Hashem* was working in *Zaidy*'s favor. My *Zaidy* was able to live through this life-threatening experience only to have many more "tests" before he came to

America. It is my belief that Hashem had better things planned for him.

Zaidy went on to marry, come to America, and have two sons and eight grandsons. Since my *Zaidy* kept his religious way of life, his sons and grandsons have continued in the fine ways to spread the words of Torah and Mitzvot throughout the Jewish community.

The Boy

Jeremy Bleiberg, Grade 11

Here he sits alone,
his thoughts have long been lost.
Nerves are frayed,
tears run free,
truly a sad sight to see.
He's given up on hope,
for it's given up on him.
He wonders why the world treats him so,
for all he'll be is a boy unknown.
And he sits alone.

His judgment has passed,
and he sits alone.
He waits for death to come,
and he sits alone.
He brings it himself,
and he sits alone.
All is silent…
And the boy is no longer alone.

The Mayor

Avi Cabessa, Grade 10

There was a mayor strong and bright,
He ruled the city day and night.
The city of New York was his rule,
He cherished the city like a jewel.
When terror struck the city's heart,
He did not falter but remained quite smart.
He led his people and kept them strong,
After evil men committed a horrid wrong.
He cried for his people that had been lost,
Firemen, policemen, what a terrible cost.
Mayor Giuliani has been around for a while,
And he graces us with his fine style.
He makes New York the city that is best,
When New York is compared to all the rest.
Mayor Giuliani is loved by all,
Too bad he hasn't been with us since the fall.

What Is

Jeremy Bleiberg, Grade 11

Heartbreak's abounding, Love's confounding.
Grief is a constant, Comfort is G-d-sent.
Sadness is draining, Happiness is…
What is Happiness?
It's indescribable with a word or phrase.
Happiness is inner peace.
Happiness is knowing that you're loved.
Happiness is a place to call home.
Happiness is…
Happiness is a much-missed dream.

The Savior

Adam Lerer, Grade 10

Every person has a savior for one thing or another.
Mine is that person we call our mother.
Day in and day out, whatever I need,
She takes care of it so I can relax and read.

Whether its English, Math, or History,
I have time to study and to play.
So much gets done with her wonderful help.
I really must stop those annoying yelps.

Every night, dinner's waiting on the table,
And on from there I go to the cable.
Eventually a few hours later,
I express my gratitude to my mother, my savior.

All my clothing she goes with me to buy,
Including that red, orange, and purple tie,
Pants, shirts, and socks for my feet,
And, sometimes, even a special treat.

These few reasons help show why I'm so thankful,
And nothing near that terrible word, "hateful."
To show my gratitude I try to exercise good behavior,
To that person I love, my mother, my savior.

Sleep

Moshe Schiffmiller, Grade 10

One of the greatest pleasures in life,
An irreplaceable ecstasy,
It passes the long hours;
It seems insufficient.

It is the meaning of bliss,
Whether with dreams or without.
It's a safe haven;
It's a sanctuary.

It beckons to you with a yawn.
A sensation beyond description,
To close your eyes
And make life melt away.

Sorrow and grief,
Gone in an instant.
Relaxation and Nirvana
Filling the void.

It's a necessity,
Often ignored,
But it will always creep up on you,
Overwhelming your consciousness.

Your abilities are impaired;
Everything's in a foggy daze.
The feeling of your pillow,
Enticing your sinking body.

There is your bed,
Lying in front of you,
Nicely made,
Inviting an occupant.

You try to resist,
A futile attempt.
The battle is lost,
But the war will go on.

Who's the Hero?

Shaul Lifshitz, Grade 12

"I have not been able to sleep lately because of an ongoing question that feels like an itch on the bottom of my foot. Is he better than I? I just can't seem to put my finger on it. I know for a fact that the answer is out there, but maybe I just haven't been looking in the right places.

"You see, he and I have this thing going that we don't really compete against each other because, in effect, we are working for the same cause. But people are always trying to compare us to see who is better, and it has finally caught up with me. I need to know. Is he better than I? It looks like what I need to do is sit down and go through fact by fact to derive an answer that is both good and true.

"Let's see now, he gets up every morning, as do I, gets dressed, as do I, and goes to work, as do I. So he gets to work, sits at his desk or whatever, and gets news from a newspaper or other source. I am the owner of an entire enterprise. I think I have the edge on that one. But then again, does having a better job make me a better man than he? If I were to say yes, then that would make me wrong for I would only be shallow and conceited, and, therefore, he would transcend in that case. However, if I were to say no, well then that just wouldn't do, now would it?

"So onward my search for a fair and better answer. When something dire calls for his attention, he leaps into action and is always there to help out in any way that he could, as do I. However, while he relies on his G-d-given talent to do things, I must rely on my own doings and the different techniques that I have acquired for myself over the years. (Now this is beginning to sound a bit more like it.) On top of that, even though he is extremely fast, extremely strong, and extremely resistant to modern-day machines of destruction, I am just a simple man, doing my job the best that I can, fending for myself in an evil world, and I might add, doing just as good a job as he does.

"I am smarter than he, more clever than he, and I, unlike him, have the common decency to dress myself in the privacy of my own home.

"I drive a much cooler car than he does (I don't even think he drives a car, does he?). And lastly, I am so much better dressed than he is. I mean spandex? In public?! And what's up with a *red* cape? Please.

"Wouldn't you agree, Alfred?"

Winter Wonderland

Shimon Rosenbaum, Grade 12

You go out for a walk on a chilly night,
The cold gripping your bones tight.
You come home and have a hot cup of tea;
You feel a warm tingly sensitivity.
The powdery snow looks like a white sheet.
It's forming into ice so slippery, so sleek.
It's best to wear gloves and warm earmuffs,
It seems the outside chill will be quite tough.

You make snow angels, moving your hands up and down.
Everybody's watching you, everyone's around.
You build snowmen with carrots, buttons and scarves.
You've been working all day; you're extremely starved.
You go home, and, with food in hand,
You realize you were playing in a winter wonderland.

Greater

Yossi Suiskind, Grade 10

I try to walk the way that I think I could
If I would only listen to myself.
I try to grope blindly for the moon in the dark of the night
When my fingertips are stars.
I doubt the feelings in my heart, for their strength is unreal.
I doubt my greatness, for I despise the egotist.
So now I am nothing, for I admit nothing to myself.
Now my eyes open, and I bask in the light of truth.

Festival of Lights

Moshe Schiffmiller, Grade 10

The flickering of the flames,
The message is sent,
Reminding us to remember,
To do teshuva and daven for a beis hamikdash,
What we sing in Maoz Tzur,
There we will sacrifice a Todah and end in song,
Our past and our future,
It is for what every Jew wishes,
The power is ours to fulfill it,
Work for it and it will come.

Meant Not to Be

Yossi Suiskind, Grade 10

Sometimes people aren't meant to be.

Light always fades in the distance.

The distance is I.

People seem to place themselves where the clouds are always blackened

And are foolishly shocked when lightning strikes, when hearts are broken.

Lightning strikes predictably where the weakened stand, where the vulnerable place themselves.

Aimless

Ben Goldman, Grade 9

I walk the streets late at night.
Death gives me an awful fright.
There is a man next to me,
Smiling there, aimlessly.
"What brings the smile there?" I say.
"Has something good come your way?
Are you wicked and hath committed wrong?
Have you been planning all along?"
I ask the man; jealously I wish to be
Smiling and so carefree.
"None of what you said is true.
I am but a humble Jew.
I've got pressing things to do."
And I look at him with envy
And I continue aimlessly.
I continue down the road…

Colder does my skin become.
I see a man drinking rum.
The man is sitting next to me,
Smiling there, aimlessly.
"What brings the smile there," I say.
"Do you live a wicked way?
Are you evil? Are you mad?
Tell me, sir! Why are you glad!"
The man then slowly looks at me,
And I look at him with much envy.
"Come, sir. I am not bad
There is a reason I'm glad!
I am but a humble man,
Believing in his own religion.
This is the cause of my smile,
Knowing life is worth the while.
Now come, sir, I beg you right,
Drink with me in this fine night!"
But I look with jealousy
And I continue aimlessly.
I continue down the road…

Time has passed and I walk more
Until I reach a glorious door.
I knock and say, "What have you here?"
I say it with a passing tear.
The man at the gate says to me,
"Have you no passing key?"
"Where can I find this key?" I say.
"Must I wander more today?"
I ask with a certain fear
That I am not welcome here.
"Must you play fool and ask?
You already failed this task!
If you had believed in me,
You would have found this golden key.
Now leave me please, let me rest,
Earth was your biggest test."
And now I wander aimlessly
And I continue down the road…

Traveler

Jeremy Bleiberg, Grade 11

Forever seems so far away
And nothing gold will ever stay.
The young and old,
The meek and bold,
The mindless and the sane,
Every day they pass me by.
Who says memories remain?

Fading Memories

Jeremy Bleiberg, Grade 11

Remember all the times we've had,
Your voice has always made me sad.
Emotions tied, connections made,
Trying hard to make them fade.
Tears are streaming down my face,
Brought by self-imposed disgrace,
Never happy, always lying,
No one seems to know I'm dying.

Football

Yaakov Strauss, Grade 11

There is one game on earth
Which is better than all.
This game brings people much mirth
And it is none other than football.

Football is a challenging game
And it is extremely fun to play.
But there is nothing that is the same
As watching pro football on Sunday.

They throw far and tackle hard;
They play rough and fight to win.
They risk being physically scarred
For the Super Bowl they're destined.

Winning and losing is part of the sport;
Teams may make it big or take a fall.
But competition is the exciting part,
And that's what's great about football.

Night

Anonymous

Its coldness warmed by the devil's whisper,
Romantic hope is its greatest lover.
Dangerous immorality is its greatest theme,
For intoxicating evil is man's favorite dream.
The moon's roar and the foretelling stars
Can in one fell swoop erase love's scars.
Night's visions shape man's heart,
For from darkness does day's light depart.

The Towers

Michael Bernstein, Grade 10

The fish in the ocean
Tell of the fall of the two,
Reflected.

The old fish
Tells the guppies
How it happened.

The blood floats on the water.
"Smoke on the water, fire in the sky"
Sings the radio,
Under.

They feel
The pain of
The fall
Of the two,
Reflected.

Identity

Moshe Schiffmiller, Grade 10

You think you know me.
You believe you know every detail about me.
The secrets I hide are nonexistent to you.
Your eyes don't see the truth.

You assume you can read me like a book.
Every page is there.
Perfect grammar and spelling make it easy to understand.
You don't realize how short the book is.

The truth is you're wrong.
Your copy of the book is missing chapters.
No human has the complete edition.
Not even me.

Idea

Moshe Schiffmiller, Grade 10

Something you can put on paper,
Something that appears in your mind,
Something difficult to express,
Something visible to the blind.

A rustling in the wind,
A fleeting elusive thought,
A glimpse into the future,
A happiness that can't be bought.

It creeps into your head,
It is not your imagination,
It disappears when wanted,
It is your best representation.

Faculty Works

פניני בינה

Stained

Sandra Schamroth Abrams, English Department

Conscious.
Like an olive tree,
You are familiar.
Gardenia musk,
Orange hues,
You are native.
Confusion. Anger. Love.
Blood stained tears.
Cuts in my mouth.
You deceived me.
I am hollow and
You've become barren.

Defense

Sandra Schamroth Abrams, English Department

Extinguish me.
Ignore me.
Incite me.
Quick vituperative tongue.
Foul stench.
Disingenuous.

Sleep, consciousness,
Ignore them.

Gentle Cooing Can Deceive

Dr. Arthur Hirshorn, Science Department

Bobbing and weaving through strollers in Rockefeller Center, or loitering around mobs of fans in front of Yankee Stadium, pigeons raise no eyebrows. Because they're so common, few New Yorkers give them more than a momentary glance.

Like New York City's human inhabitants, pigeons must also contend with air pollution, noise, rush-hour traffic and a landscape covered predominantly by concrete and asphalt. Yet in several significant ways, the Big Apple is hospitable to these birds.

First of all, there are very few natural predators for pigeons to worry about. The few peregrine falcons spotted on Manhattan office buildings are no threat to their survival. Second, there are more than enough sheltered lofts and nest sites throughout the cityscape. Finally, with plenty of food available all year, migration is unnecessary.

The pigeon is a native of the rocky coastlines along north Africa and southern Europe. It is also known as the rock dove because it makes evening shelters (called lofts) and nests within the nooks and crannies of eroded cliffs. In our town, pigeons find ideal nests and lofts in the elaborate façades of churches, synagogues and older buildings. In fact, any tall structure—elevated subway stations, highway overpasses and rafters of outdoor stadiums—with numerous concealed spaces (known as "pigeon holes") is irresistible to breeding rock doves.

More than 5,000 years ago, dwellings in Egypt and Mesopotamia were constructed with special nesting boxes called dovecotes designed to attract pigeons. Since pigeons always return home, dovecote owners were supplied with a regular bounty of fresh eggs and tender youth squab. The homing instinct of pigeons was responsible for an early form of "air mail/special delivery." The legions of ancient Rome routinely took along carrier pigeons whenever they left for extended tours, especially to the distant lands of northwestern Europe. Roman commanders were able to communicate with the emperor by attaching messages to the legs of swift-flying pigeons.

Adult pigeons are strictly herbivorous. However, they feed their nestlings numerous insects and worms. Unquestionably, the animal protein contained within the bodies of earthworms, caterpillars and insect larvae influences the rapid growth of newborn pigeons. Within three weeks, juvenile pigeons are almost as large as their parents. Perhaps this explains why you'll rarely see a baby pigeon.

Sidewalks, curbsides and shopping malls are popular pigeon feeding areas, especially near delicatessens and pizza parlors. Here, they feast upon discarded pizza crusts and the overbaked ends of frankfurter rolls. However, one of the very best places to watch pigeons en masse is around the park bench. Seated, with their paper or plastic shopping bags filled with breadcrumbs and birdseed, senior citizens ensure the daily appearance of pigeons by the hundreds.

Since the pigeon or dove has long been portrayed as a symbol of peace, it surprises many people to see how aggressive they really are.

For example, to keep the smaller, quicker house sparrow from eating sidewalk edibles, pigeons push them away with their muscular wings and block access with their plump bodies. Moreover, the wing-fighting and pecking characteristic of competing male suitors is especially savage.

On busy downtown sidewalks, New Yorkers walk around pigeons without a hint of curiosity, while taxi drivers, careening cross-town, make sharp turns into flocks of them, as if they weren't there. Fortunately—for the pigeons—their reflexes and peripheral vision are keen, enabling them to hop up on the curb or take to the air in the knick of time.

But pigeons, especially those breeding on ledges or windowsills, make some New Yorkers indignant. Besides the mess they make, their repetitious early-morning moaning can transform mild-mannered people into wide-eyed, broom-toting pigeon stalkers. And let's not forget about those well-dressed bankers, lawyers and doctors who curse pigeons for ruining their expensive suits. My advice: avoid buildings' "drip line," and always carry an umbrella when walking beneath elevated subway stations.

In general, birds will not permit a human observer to approach any closer than ten feet. Even the cosmopolitan house sparrow and starling take off when pedestrians get too close. However, the pigeon is one bird you don't need a pair of binoculars to observe. In fact, this plump-bodied, small-headed relative of the dodo will practically bump into you on its scavenger hunts throughout the city.

Untitled

Erik Huber, Faculty, English Department

When I heard that a plane hit the Twin Towers I thought: small plane, surely, and few dead, surely, because they are not mere buildings, like those in Belgrade or Hiroshima. This is the World Trade Center, the modern Stonehenge, the Druid god keeping watch over the vigorous disciples of global capitalism, plus the objects of their exploitation in the five boroughs and parts of New Jersey, and even over my own building. Often in the warmer months I would climb to the roof at night and gaze in wonder at these pillars of light floating alone and close in the dark sky like disinterested alien beings, visible markers of my proximity to the power and the glamour of Manhattan. Somehow the buildings must be able to repel mere jets, I thought, with their magic silvery aura of absolute authority.

I climbed to the roof and discovered my neighborhood engulfed in a cloud of thick, toxic white smoke, the streets below quiet and empty save for a stream of solitary commuters, briefcases in hand, ties over their shoulders. They were walking with their customary swift determination, but they were headed home at 9:30 a.m., and covered with ashes. None of them looked back as the Towers and thousands of their occupants dissolved into particulate matter. At that moment I felt ripped free of all the preoccupations that had governed my morning and delved into solitary existential truth. Death was present. Mortality and its attendant realities – vulnerability, decline, the tenderness of flesh.

We spend every waking moment strategizing to evade certain realities, certain inevitabilities. We ride the exercise bicycle like caged hamsters ride the wheel, we arm ourselves with arsenals of vitamins and pills, we eat oatmeal, we build our stock portfolios or our grade point averages or our office towers so high that from an office at the top it is not hard to believe one has risen from the common fate that awaits us all.

And while we strategize thus, there are these terrorists who devote their lives to an opposite line of thinking. While we seek to imagine ourselves safe, they seek ways to prove us vulnerable. While we imagine our buildings magic and eternal, they understand that anything built by men can be dismantled by men. While we try to imagine that our nuclear and biological weapons are securely in the grip of capable hands, the terrorist asks…are they? Is this in fact so?

Now we are all forced to think in this respect as they do. We are aware of our vulnerability, and more wary of the hubris that assumes that anything we create with the intention of destruction will always remain under the control of rational minds. We are more aware that danger lies in the sufferings of others because they are capable of making us suffer with them. Any place in the world where people lack real opportunities, lack the dignity of self government, suffer because they are Jews, or because they are Arabs, or because they are Muslims, or because they are under the thumb of an autocratic government propped up by ours, we have to have our eyes open. We have to be aware. Denial is dangerous.

Remember

Sandra Schamroth Abrams, English Department

Steady and even
Warm breath.
Hairs rise on the back of my neck.

Light drizzle and gentle taps
Draw me inward.
Te recuerdo.

Obscure paths merging:
The unknown familiar.

Open mouth, inhaling
Perfumed memories,
Feverish, exact.
Quiero recordar!

Facing Tragedy?

Sandra Schamroth Abrams, English Department

Self-effacing vulnerability
Millennium joys no longer easy
I can't sleep
How small my world is
I want to dream
I want to bleed
Any guiltless normalcy

These Birds Are No Angels

Dr. Arthur Hirshorn, Science Department

At less than six inches from beak to tail, and rarely weighing more than an ounce, the house sparrow is clearly no heavyweight. But, gram for gram, these chunky little avians are among the most aggressive and visible residents of New York City.

Although often called the English sparrow, this bird is neither a native of England, nor is it a sparrow. In fact, it's a member of the Ploceidae, a family of finches native to Africa and the Middle East. However, since it was introduced from England to Brooklyn in 1850, it has been known to many generations of New Yorkers as the English sparrow.

House sparrows are classified as perching birds. Members placed within this order—ranging from the tiny goldfinch to the conspicuous crow—possess a distinctive toe and tendon arrangement. When a perching bird supports its weight upon a tree branch, utility wire or clothesline, the three front toes and large hind ones grasp the perch and "lock." This enables the house sparrow, as well as your pet canary, to rest or sleep while standing.

The body temperature of a house sparrow matches its hot-headed disposition, averaging a whopping 108 degrees Fahrenheit. To maintain such a high level of body heat, it burns calories at a rate more than 300 times greater than a human being. Not surprisingly, these high-strung birds eat incessantly.

The house sparrow's short, thick beak is perfect for cracking and shelling small seeds. The birds' predominantly "grainiferous" diet has not endeared them to farms, as they readily eat corn, wheat and oats. But, their consumption of the seeds of lawn-invading weeds, such as dandelion and ragweed, does make life a little easier for the urban gardener and hay fever sufferer.

In the mid-nineteenth century, house sparrows were regularly seen following horse carriages around town, feasting upon the undigested oats that invariably trailed behind them. In retrospect, a more appropriate name for these chunky finches would have been "horse" sparrows. In any case, with the emergence of the horseless carriage, the adaptable house sparrow merely focused more attention on the increasing volume of sidewalk edibles and abundant weeds found in public parks and vacant lots.

Noteworthy is a moniker that the English have used to describe the house sparrow: "little hoodlum."

House sparrows cannot resist stealing food from pigeons. Brazen house sparrows regularly dart into groups of feeding pigeons, emerging with oversized pieces of bread protruding form their beaks.

Worse, the house sparrow has a nasty habit of raiding and appropriating the nests of other small birds. Finding a suitable unattended nest, a little hoodlum will destroy the eggs or push out the helpless nestlings and use these sites for raising its own progeny.

For this reason, ornithologists claim that the pugnacious house sparrow has played a major role in the retreat of native songbirds, such as the blue bird and the purple marten, from New York City during this century.

While urban living has greatly reduced the threat of predation by hawks, falcons and owls, house sparrows are not without enemies. Throughout the breeding season, house sparrows must be vigilant against marauding crows, bluejays and tree squirrels, which prey on their eggs and nestlings. A convincing example of the house sparrow's pugnacity is the sight of one of these fearless birds chasing a two-foot-long crow from the vicinity of its nest.

Unlike those other urban birds, the pigeon and the starling, the male and female house sparrow are colored differently. Males have a noticeable black "bib," slate-gray crown, white wing bars and chestnut-brown patches on their heads and backs. In comparison, the females' pale-gray and light brown plumage appears washed out.

The house sparrow's home is easy to spot. Just proceed to any busy intersection in mid-Manhattan and look up. You'll see an example of the house sparrow's adaptable nature. In their aggressive search for nest sites, they have adopted the small, hollow cylinders of crossties that support traffic lights around town. Here, 10 to 15 feet above the congested streets of one of the world's largest cities, the house sparrow has found a perfect fit.

Printed in the United States
4499